World War II in Alaska

ALASKA GEOGRAPHIC / Volume 22, Number 4

To teach many more to better know and more wisely use our natural resources...

EDITOR
Penny Rennick

PRODUCTION DIRECTOR
Kathy Doogan

STAFF WRITER
L.J. Campbell

BOOKKEEPER/DATABASE MANAGER
Vickie Staples

MARKETING MANAGER
Pattey Parker Mancini

POSTMASTER: Send address changes to
ALASKA GEOGRAPHIC®
P.O. Box 93370
Anchorage, Alaska 99509-3370

PRINTED IN U.S.A.

ISBN: 1-56661-028-1

Price to non-members this issue: $19.95

ALASKA GEOGRAPHIC® (ISSN 0361-1353) is published quarterly by The Alaska Geographic Society, 639 West International Airport Road, Unit 38, Anchorage, AK 99518. Second-class postage paid at Anchorage, Alaska, and additional mailing offices. Copyright © 1996 by The Alaska Geographic Society. All rights reserved. Registered trademark: Alaska Geographic, ISSN 0361-1353; Key title Alaska Geographic.

THE ALASKA GEOGRAPHIC SOCIETY is a non-profit, educational organization dedicated to improving geographic understanding of Alaska and the North, putting geography back in the classroom and exploring new methods of teaching and learning.

MEMBERS receive *ALASKA GEOGRAPHIC*®, a quality publication that devotes each quarterly issue to monographic in-depth coverage of a northern geographic region or resource-oriented subject.

MEMBERSHIP in The Alaska Geographic Society costs $39 per year, $49 to non-U.S. addresses. ($31.20 of the membership fee is for a one-year subscription to *ALASKA GEOGRAPHIC*®.) Order from: Alaska Geographic Society, Box 93370, Anchorage, AK 99509-3370; phone (907) 562-0164, fax (907) 562-0479.

SUBMITTING PHOTOGRAPHS: Please write for a list of upcoming topics or other specific photo needs and a copy of our editorial guidelines. We cannot be responsible for unsolicited submissions. Submissions not accompanied by sufficient postage for return by certified mail will be returned by regular mail.

CHANGE OF ADDRESS: The post office does not automatically forward *ALASKA GEOGRAPHIC*® when you move. To ensure continuous service, please notify us at least six weeks before moving. Send your new address and your membership number or a mailing label from a recent *ALASKA GEOGRAPHIC*® to: The Alaska Geographic Society, P.O. Box 93370, Anchorage, AK 99509-3370.

COLOR SEPARATIONS: Graphic Chromatics

PRINTED BY: The Hart Press

The Library of Congress has cataloged this serial publication as follows:

Alaska Geographic. v.1-
[Anchorage, Alaska Geographic Society] 1972-
v. ill. (part col.). 23 x 31 cm.
Quarterly
Official publication of The Alaska Geographic Society.
Key title: Alaska geographic, ISSN 0361-1353.

1. Alaska—Description and travel—1959-
—Periodicals. I. Alaska Geographic Society.

F901.A266 917.98'04'505 72-92087

Library of Congress 75[79112] MARC-S

COVER: *In August 1943, U.S. and Canadian soldiers display a Japanese flag left behind on Kiska Island. This photo has been colorized. (U.S. Government photo, courtesy of Jack Haugen)*

PREVIOUS PAGE: *A Japanese gun emplacement overlooks Kiska Harbor and Little Kiska Island in the western Aleutians. (Edward Steele)*

FACING PAGE: *Cape Chiniak was an important defensive position to protect Kodiak, where the Navy, Army and Army Air Force established their joint command center. In time Kodiak grew into the largest naval base in Alaska during World War II. (John Tuckey)*

About This Issue: As the United States celebrates the 50th anniversary of the end of World War II, it seems only appropriate that *ALASKA GEOGRAPHIC*® devote an issue to some of the events from 1940 to 1945 that brought the war home to Alaskans. The entire territory mobilized for the war effort, and when hostilities ceased, Alaskans were left with a changed Alaska, more people, more roads, better communications, and perhaps most of all a better sense of what Alaska meant to the rest of the country.

For this issue, we thank the researchers who have helped compile our nation's military history, in particular John Haile Cloe, historian and author at Elmendorf Air Force Base; D. Colt Denfeld of the U.S. Army Corps of Engineers; and Ted Spencer of the Alaska Aviation Heritage Museum. For assistance with photos and biographical notes of prominent Alaskans and World War II figures, we thank Lynn Binek of the Anchorage Museum Association; Mary Lou Gjernes of the Center of Military History in Washington D.C.; Richard Van Cleve, registrar, Tongass Historical Museum; Mike Clark of the Naval Historical Center in Washington D.C.; Margaret Weatherly of Reeve Aleutian Airways; Bob Wrentmore of Morrison Knudsen Corp. and Dr. Jeanne Culbertson, formerly of Adak and now of New Mexico.

Above all, we thank the veterans of World War II, many of whom wrote us and kindly shared their memories and photos of that important time a half-century ago. We especially thank Jack Haugen of Arizona, who educated us on the PBYs and the men who flew them. We are grateful to Hiroichi Samejima, Wylie Hunt and Luke Watkins, who agreed to talk with reporter Rob Carson of *The News Tribune* in Tacoma, Wash. about their experiences in the Aleutians; and to Harold K. Saur, whose photos and diary brought to light a seldom-publicized expedition to the North Slope in search of oil in 1944. The overview article was written by staff writer, L.J. Campbell. Information about the authors of the other articles is contained in the editorial notes preceding each article.

Contents

Arsenal of Democracy

By L.J. Campbell

Anyone who has driven the Alaska Highway, flown into King Salmon or Cold Bay, boarded a boat in Whittier, or explored oceanfront parklands in Seward has encountered some of Alaska's World War II legacy.

In fact, much of what one finds in Alaska today is linked in some way to World War II.

For a brief period in the early 1940s, Alaska was the continent's northernmost defense during World War II. Thousands of military personnel and civilian construction crews moved in, and millions of dollars were spent building airfields, sea ports and bases the size of small cities. Residents rallied in grassroots allegiance to protect their homeland; the Alaska Territorial Guard of mostly Natives and a sea patrol rescue unit of mostly Alaska fishermen were two of several groups formed with local citizens.

Wartime alliances forged between the United States and Canada led to joint Air Force operations in Alaska and brought about construction of the Alaska Highway and a fuel pipeline through Canada. Alaska also served as the main transfer point for airplanes, ships, ammunition and supplies headed to the Soviet Union as part of America's Lend-Lease program.

And in one of the most overlooked campaigns of World War II, Alaska saw actual battle.

The only fighting on North American soil during the war took place in Alaska's Aleutian Islands. The Japanese bombed Dutch Harbor and invaded Attu and Kiska islands in June 1942. Soon after, a small U.S. naval fleet defeated a more powerful Japanese armada in the Komandorski Islands west of the Aleutians, choking enemy attempts to resupply the occupied islands. Through 1943, American air and naval forces bombed and shelled the Japanese on Attu and Kiska, finally retaking Attu in a bloody amphibious assault. Landing troops stormed Kiska, too, firing through the fog at what turned out to be each other, not knowing that the enemy had secretly abandoned the island weeks before.

Then in the final months of war, air bases in the western Aleutians launched bombing raids against the Japanese-held Kurile Islands.

This wreck of B-24D Liberator 41-2367 is a reminder of the kind of mishaps that can occur during war times and of how much havoc bad weather can cause for flyers. This particular misadventure, however, has a happy ending. On Dec. 9, 1942, this bomber from the 404th Bombardment Squadron, flown by captains John Andrews and Louis Blau with passengers Brig. Gen. William Lynch and Col. John V. Hart, was on weather patrol from Adak to Attu. Lynch, inspector general for Gen. "Hap" Arnold, wanted to see firsthand what difficulties the Eleventh Air Force was encountering with Aleutian weather. On the return trip, the plane was weathered out at Adak and headed for neighboring Atka Island. The landing field there was not yet complete and the plane was low on fuel. The pilots followed the north shore of Atka, debating whether to ditch in the water or try for a belly landing on the tundra. They opted for land and slid 150 yards across the turf. The general suffered a cracked collarbone, but the others aboard survived more or less intact. The following night the seaplane tender Gillis picked up the passengers and crew. As of late 1995 the bomber still rested on Atka's tundra. (Lon E. Lauber)

Lives were tragically lost in fighting, but also in the stormy weather that battered the Aleutians. Even the most routine daily flying patrols became dangerous survival missions in the fog-enshrouded, mountainous islands.

Caught on the battlefield were the Aleuts, the Native inhabitants of the islands. Invaded by the military from both sides, their villages were destroyed and their lives forever changed. Some of them were captured and taken to Japan as prisoners; others were evacuated by the U.S. government to dismal internment camps in Southeast Alaska.

Yet few World War II histories mention Alaska – the battles waged here, the sacrifices its people made, or the role it played in the northern line of defense as war raged through the Pacific.

Perhaps the omission of how war came to Alaska is understandable. World War II was a global event. What started in Europe in 1939, when Germany invaded Poland, escalated into the largest armed conflict ever waged on Earth. It involved every major world power, pitting the Allies led by England, France and the United States against the Axis aggressors, Germany, Japan and Italy. While Adolph Hitler marched his German Nazis through Europe into Russia, Japan drove into East Asia and through the Pacific. The United States officially joined the war in

World War II in Alaska

(*ALASKA GEOGRAPHIC*® map by Kathy Doogan)

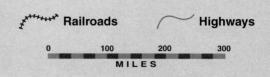

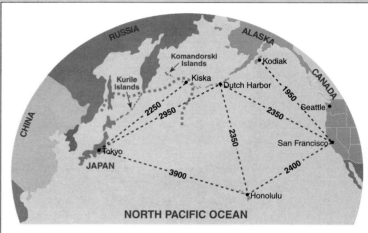

World War II on the Pacific Rim

•••••• **Extent of Japanese expansion in Alaska**
- - - - - - **Distances between points, in statute miles**

(**Source:** *Distances Between Ports*, U.S. Govt. Pub. 151, Defense Mapping Agency, 1995)

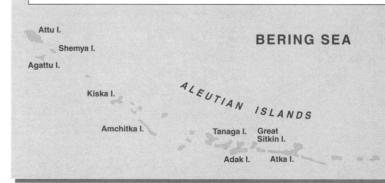

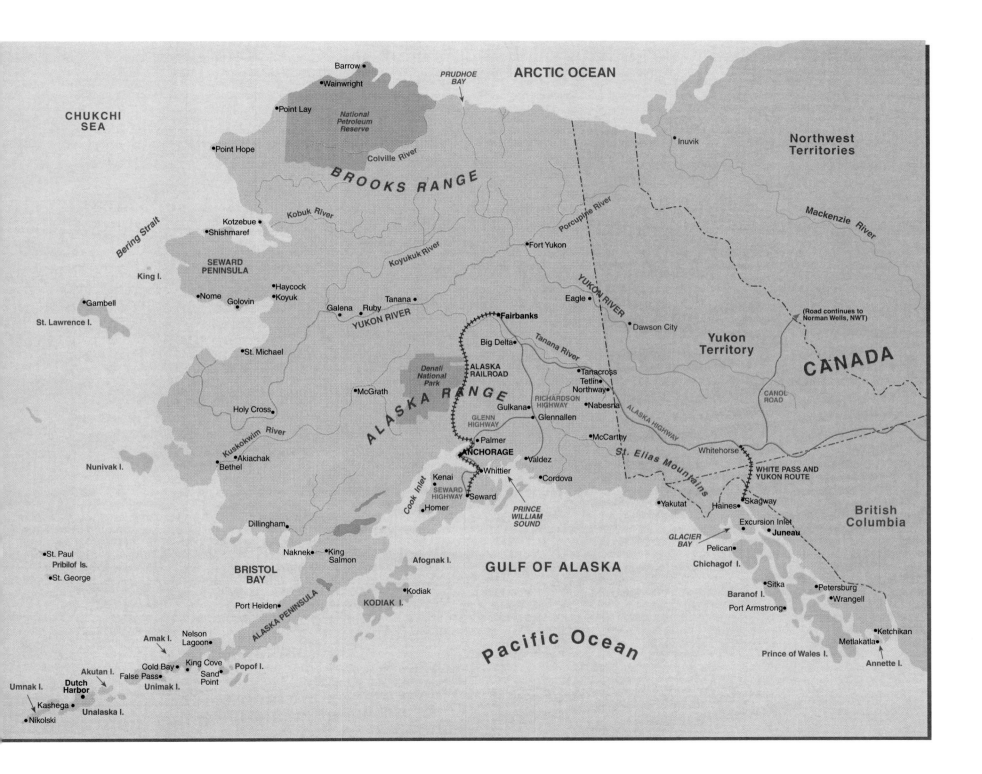

December 1941, after Japan bombed the American naval base at Pearl Harbor in Hawaii. Fighting came to Alaska the following June.

In the overall scheme of World War II and compared to other combat theaters, Alaska played only a small part militarily. The Aleutian campaign amounted to a minor diversion that briefly tied up some of Japan's troops, ships and planes, preventing them from being deployed elsewhere. It did result in recovery of an intact Japanese Zero fighter plane, the first time the enemy's superior weapon was available for Allied scrutiny; the rebuilt Zero was used to train American fliers in combat strategy. And the Lend-

Lease program aided by Alaska helped Russia withstand German takeover, although it's unclear to what extent.

Given this, that Alaska was a footnote in the larger World War II annals, the war nevertheless played a huge part in bringing about the Alaska that we know today.

The Alaska Highway, built as a military road, is still the only way to drive in and out of most of the state without putting your vehicle on a boat. Cold Bay and King Salmon, built as air bases, are just two of many Alaska towns that owe their existence to the military. The port town of Whittier, for instance, was

One of the major building projects in western North America during World War II was construction of the Alaska Highway (Alcan) from Dawson Creek, British Columbia to Big Delta in Alaska's Interior, where the route joined with the Richardson Highway and continued on into Fairbanks. More than 11,000 troops, many of whom were African Americans, from several engineering regiments, were assigned to punch through a road as an alternative in case the Japanese cut sea-going supply routes. The 1,500-mile highway remains the only land connection between most of Alaska and the continental highway system. (Alissa Crandall)

built as a secret military fuel depot and alternate sea route, in case the main port at Seward was bombed by the enemy. Caines Head State Recreation Area near Seward, one of several historical war sites in the state, commemorates coastal defense installations aimed at protecting that port and railroad terminal.

The war spurred significant boosts to Alaska's population, an upward spiral that gave momentum to eventual statehood. The recognition of Alaska as a northern defensive outpost led to increased military spending here after the war, as former World War II bases were enlarged into the nation's foremost northern defense uniÉ© of the Cold War. Today, military spending continues to be important to Alaska's economy, particularly in cities such as Anchorage and Fairbanks where major bases are located.

Without question, World War II brought pervasive changes of long-lasting consequence to Alaska. The impact and changes wrought by Alaska's war years are comparable in scope to Russian rule in early Alaska and then more recently, the era of Alaska the oil state, as defined by the Prudhoe Bay oil strike and construction of the trans-Alaska pipeline.

Now let's look closer at Alaska's war years.

On the Eve of War

Relatively few people lived in Alaska in the years immediately preceding the territory's fortification.

The 1939 census counted 72,524 residents, almost half of whom were Natives. More than 20 percent of the territory's population lived in five Southeast towns; the largest town in the territory was the capital city of Juneau with 5,720 people. The second largest was Ketchikan, with Anchorage in Southcentral and Fairbanks in the Interior ranked third and fourth, respectively. More than 60 percent of the territory's residents lived scattered about in remote villages, camps, and fishing, mining and logging enclaves.

No doubt soldiers working on construction of the Alaska Highway (Alcan) in 1942 expressed sentiments similar to this roadside philosopher at Tetsa River Services, Mile 357.5 of the highway in British Columbia. (Alissa Crandall)

Salmon fishing drove the territory's economy, accounting for about 80 percent of the tax revenues. The fishing industry was controlled mostly by outsiders, primarily from Seattle, who operated the canneries and shipping lines. Gold mining still supported Juneau, Fairbanks and Nome. Anchorage was mostly a railroad town, having been born in 1915 as headquarters for construction of the federal Alaska Railroad, then the largest public works project in Alaska.

The railroad was the main transportation artery through Southcentral, from tidewater at the port city of Seward, north through Anchorage to Fairbanks. The only road inland from the sea was the Richardson Highway, from Valdez on Prince William Sound to Fairbanks. Alaskans still depended on boats and ships for coastal commerce around the territory and beyond.

Airplanes were, however, gaining in importance. The first small airline companies in the territory started out of Ketchikan and Fairbanks in the 1920s and by the 1930s, the Civil Aeronautics Authority was regulating commercial flight. In 1938, the CAA started building airfields around Alaska, to give pilots something better than cleared strips of wilderness.

U.S. Coast Guard and Navy personnel pack explosives to an ammunition dump during a typical fog-blanketed Aleutian day. Weather was as much the enemy as were the Japanese during the Aleutian campaign. Fog, wind, rain and snow made flying conditions treacherous. The weather provided cover for the Japanese task force as it steamed away from Unalaska Island after bombing Dutch Harbor. It also helped the Japanese remove their large force from Kiska Island after the Battle of Attu. (Lon E. Lauber)

Aviation would play an important role in Alaska's wartime development.

Strategically Poised

Alaska's strategic position in the north had been noted by various forward-thinkers for years.

As early as 1867, Sec. of State William Seward opined that whoever controlled Alaska would control the North Pacific. He convinced Congress to purchase Alaska from Russia, but few others recognized its value and the acquisition became popularly known as Seward's Folly.

The Navy had surveyed the Aleutian Islands for trade route possibilities during Russian rule, but did not consider the islands' military potential until 1904, when it acquired land to build a coaling station on Kiska Island. The project died with no construction a few years later for lack of money.

In the early 1900s, territorial Gov. John Brady requested more Navy gunboat patrols. Along the coast, Japanese fishing boats were moving closer to shore bothering Alaska fishermen, and Brady was worried. He also called for coastal defenses at Dutch Harbor; the Navy built a communications station there in 1911.

Territorial delegate James Wickersham tried in 1921 to persuade the Navy to build a major base in Homer.

In 1920, another proponent of Alaska's strategic importance set forth to prove the point with aviation. Army Air Service Brig. Gen. William Mitchell, a prophet of military air might, sent four planes from New York to Nome. Mitchell had commanded installation of telegraph lines between Valdez and Eagle in 1901, part of the Washington Alaska Military Cable and Telegraph System (WAMCATS). He saw Alaska as one of the "most strategic places in the world" because of its location, and he predicted that unfriendly forces might someday try to use Alaska as an invasion route into North America. Advances in aviation technology were finally making long-distance flight possible, something Mitchell wanted to show with the 1920 expedition, 9,000 miles round-trip. He was convinced that air power would be the key to military strength, particularly in Alaska, the air crossroads of the North Pacific.

Another two decades would pass before Mitchell's vision would be fully recognized, although others would take up his call as world unrest heightened after World War I. Political instability plagued Europe, revolutions shook governments in Russia, China, the Middle East and Japan, and economies collapsed worldwide.

In 1931 Japan occupied Manchuria, signaling the expansionist intent of Japan's controlling military. Then Japan withdrew from an arms limitation treaty with the United States and started building its navy. The United States likewise began reevaluating its military preparedness in the Pacific.

The working blueprint for America's defense was found in color-coded plans—one dealing with Germany, another with Japan—which had been formulated after World War I by a joint Army-Navy board. Alaska was not mentioned in the early plans but by the 1930s, Army and Navy defense planners were beginning to consider Alaska's role in a Pacific theater of war.

The remote and vast territory was largely undefended. In the years following the purchase of Alaska and through the turn-of-the-century gold rush, Navy gunboats and Army troops had governed. But in the 1920s, most of the military withdrew. The Navy still conducted limited sea patrols and occasional charting surveys. U.S. Army Signal Corps personnel manned remote telegraph stations scattered about the territory, but by 1925, the territory's only Army base was Chilkoot Barracks, a foreign duty post outside Haines with 300 rifle-toting soldiers.

The military would clearly need a bigger presence if Alaska was to figure strategically.

Territorial delegate Anthony Dimond spoke loudly of this need. He questioned the military's decision to fortify the Hawaiian Islands and not Alaska, which he likened to leaving the back door open. He sponsored an unsuccessful bill to build Army and Navy bases in the territory.

Between 1931 and 1936, the Navy sent four survey expeditions into the Aleutians and held Pacific fleet exercises in the islands in 1935. But the resulting reports of strong winds, fog, rain, stormy seas and mountainous terrain painted the Aleutians as most uninviting for naval seaplane operations, with little flat land suitable for land-based planes. In 1937, the Navy built a small air station at Sitka in Southeast, where training missions had been held several years previously.

Dear Editor:

Enjoyed your letter giving me a rundown of Yakutat where I spent from January 1942 to early 1943. I was on the little diesel engine that ran from the cannery to Lost River. In 1942 they said the railroad belonged to Libby, McNeil & Libby, who owned the cannery and general store in town.

I remember an intelligent gentleman who lived year-round on a small boat with a cabin. I can't recall his last name, but his first name was George and he graduated from Dartmouth College. The Army employed George and if we had to leave by foot, he knew a path over the St. Elias Mountains.

I also remember a runway for bombers, fighters and other plans. It was one of the largest runways I had ever seen. Of course, we couldn't mention it in any correspondence.

We left Yakutat in March or April of 1943 for Attu. There were only the Japanese when we landed on Attu. Their last bit of action was sometime in October when they conducted a heavy bomber mission on the island, probably from an aircraft carrier or Paramushiro. On Army maps Attu is called Camp Earle as Colonel Earle was the first high-ranking officer killed on Attu.

—*Thomas V. McNutt*
Oreland, Pa.

The tundra held many surprises for attacking ground troops, not the least of which were these anti-personnel stakes left on Adak Island. (Lon E. Lauber)

Then in 1937, Japan invaded China. U.S. relations with Japan further deteriorated when Japan bombed an American gunboat on China's Yangtze River. In Europe, tensions worsened as Adolph Hitler rose to power in Germany.

A report outlining the U.S. Navy's needs for national defense, submitted to Congress in 1938 by Rear Adm. Arthur J. Hepburn, contained the first significant budget for Alaska, although a paltry one compared to the Navy's spending in Hawaii and elsewhere. A $19 million defense project in Alaska called for enlarging the Sitka base and building seaplane and submarine bases at Kodiak and Dutch Harbor.

Meanwhile, the Army decided to build a cold-weather testing facility in Fairbanks, to train pilots and develop equipment for arctic conditions. It was Alaska's first Army airfield, and the only one in Alaska included in a larger package of Army airfields nationwide authorized by Congress in 1934. Construction on Ladd Field started five years later, when its $4 million cost was finally funded.

The Army also was charged with protecting naval installations on the coast, with garrisons of Army troops, airplanes and pilots. It selected Anchorage as its Alaska headquarters for Army and Army Air

operations, and withdrew 43,495 acres for the site. But Congress refused to fund the Anchorage Army base, questioning its need in addition to Ladd Field and the seaplane base in Kodiak.

But soon afterward, the mood in Congress changed. Germany invaded Poland in fall of '39, then swiftly took Norway, Denmark, Holland, Belgium and France. In the Pacific, Japan continued her aggressions. When Japan signed a neutrality pact with Germany and Italy, U.S. leaders feared a second world war was inevitable.

The nation readied itself. Factories retooled to produce ships, planes and ammunition. Young men signed up for the nation's first ever peacetime draft. The Navy reinforced its fleet at Pearl Harbor, and Congress stopped debating the need for military bases in Alaska.

In May 1940, Congress appropriated money for Army bases in Anchorage and Army coastal defenses at Kodiak and Dutch Harbor. The fortification of Alaska was underway.

Here Come the Troops

Civilian construction crews, equipment, supplies and troops surged into Alaska. First to Anchorage, to Kodiak, to Dutch Harbor and Sitka – the primary military stations. Then as the buildup escalated, to Nome, Bethel, McGrath, Naknek and Sand Point – sites chosen for forward Army and Navy air bases. To Cordova, Yakutat, Metlakatla, and Annette Island – for seaplane bases and airfields. To Cold Bay on the Alaska Peninsula and Umnak Island in the Aleutians – for secret Army airfields to defend the Navy at Dutch Harbor. To Tanana Crossing, Galena, Fort Yukon, Ruby, Big Delta and Northway - for intermediate airfields needed to ferry planes to the forward bases. And in the height of the Aleutian campaign, to Adak, Amchitka, Shemya and other

Beach greens grow through Marston mats, which were laid as temporary runways in the Aleutians during the war. The field at Otter Point on Umnak Island required an initial 80,000 sections of Marston mat. The mat was developed by the Army and tried out first in November 1941 near Marston, N.C. To be useful, the mat had to be easily assembled, a task that usually fell to the infantry. Each section weighed a little more than 66 pounds, was 10 feet by 15 inches, and covered 12.5 square feet. (Lon E. Lauber) western islands for harbors and airfields to push the enemy out.

More than 300 military installations would be built in Alaska, at a cost of more than $350 million, before the war was through.

The scene was similar in each location. Tents went up for the first workers, who unloaded lumber, machinery and food arriving by ship, rail or plane. With a flurry of earth moving and pile driving, roads and runways, docks, warehouses and barracks, power and water plants went in. Troops arrived, units of national guardsmen, engineers, infantry and field artillery regiments from places as far away as West Virginia, Alabama, Missouri. For many, the rough voyage to Alaska was their first time at sea. But in Alaska they got overseas duty pay, a welcome bonus; regular pay at the time for privates was $1 a day.

Local villages and towns swarmed with strange faces and the sound of change; jobs abounded with the contractors, the military and new businesses opening in response to the burgeoning population. Even the most remote communities, like King Island in the Bering Sea, felt the effects of the military economy. Eskimo women there sewed sealskin mukluks to sell to sailors on ships anchored offshore, and longshoring jobs with the military in Nome drew the young men away from their traditional life.

Yet living conditions were bleak for many soldiers, particularly those in the Aleutians where tents routinely sailed away in the swirling winds, collapsed in the rain, sank in the mud; where meagerly fueled stoves and inadequate clothing did little against the penetrating cold; where many a bored, fearful or homesick soldier swigged "Aleutian Solution" homebrew for comfort. The military waged many battles in Alaska, not all of them against the Japanese.

In the commanding ranks, personality clashes and jurisdictional jealousies threatened Alaska's defense as well.

The territory was part of the Army's Western Defense Command, headquartered in San Francisco under Gen. John DeWitt. He assigned Col. Simon Bolivar Buckner Jr. to command the newly created Alaska Defense Force, and Buckner arrived in Anchorage in July 1940 to oversee the territory's fortification. He was soon promoted to general.

A West Point graduate, Buckner came from distinguished southern military heritage. He was dynamic and energetic, aggressive and outspoken to

LEFT:
The Japanese built this 1,200-foot pier into Kiska Harbor during their occupation of this western Aleutian island in 1942-1943. (Edward Steele)

ABOVE:
Ken Goe holds a spent casing from a Japanese gun. (Edward Steele)

RIGHT:
The calm of this scene of Iliuliuk Bay and Dutch Harbor belies the fury of the Japanese attack 53 years ago. Abandoned Quonset huts, gun emplacements, bunkers and other reminders of the conflict dot the tundra-covered slopes above the bay. (Harry M. Walker)

BELOW:
Among the relics of World War II are these 20mm incendiary rounds weathering away in the tundra of Tanaga Island. (Lon E. Lauber)

the extreme. He did not want black soldiers stationed in Alaska, and he barred Native women from entering United Service Organization (USO) clubs. He was not censured for his racism; the times were different then. (After leaving Alaska in June 1944, he commanded the U.S. 10th Army at Okinawa, where he was killed, on June 18, 1945, on the front lines; he was the highest ranking officer to be killed in combat in the Pacific theater.)

Buckner was powerful. With a budget 100 times greater that of the territorial legislature's $3 million, he got much of what he wanted, notes historian Jonathan Nielson in *Armed Forces on a Northern Frontier* (1988). Buckner needed heavy machinery for base construction and convinced the legislature to

suspend mining as an unnecessary wartime activity, then called all the equipment into military use. He ordered Mount McKinley National Park to be used exclusively by the military for rest and relaxation. He resourcefully manipulated the system to achieve his ends, when Washington was slow to respond. He decided where airfields were needed and ordered them built, diverting money and supplies from one to another until his new directives were authorized.

Where land ended, though, Alaska fell into other hands. In 1941, Rear Adm. Robert Theobald arrived in Alaska to command the Navy's small North Pacific Force. Theobald was as cautious as Buckner was daring. Distrustful and condescending, he was described as "one of the best brains and worst dispositions in the Navy." Theobald and Buckner did not get along. During the Aleutian campaign, considered a naval engagement, Theobald was put in charge. Buckner, who had directed the territory's buildup and did not agree with Theobald's tactics, resented being subordinate. Their festering discord was a contributing factor to Theobald's replacement in 1943 with Rear Adm. Thomas C. Kinkaid, who struck a congenial working relationship with Buckner.

Meanwhile, the Army's Eleventh Air Force commanded by Gen. William O. Butler, was at the disposal of both the Army and Navy. The rivalry that grew between Theobald and Buckner complicated Butler's job considerably.

Another important figure during Alaska's war years was Col. Benjamin Talley, commander of the Army Corps of Engineers. Talley's first project was designing and building the Yakutat airfield. With its swift completion by the end of 1940, Talley was then put in charge of all Army construction projects on the mainland, including construction of Army airfields and Army coastal defenses on naval installations. The Navy's early projects, as well as some of the Army coastal garrisons, were started by civilian contractors such as Morrison-Knudsen or Siems Drake Puget Sound, and finished by Naval Construction Battalions (Seabees) or Army Corps engineers under Talley's oversight.

Many of the airfields in Alaska were started by the Civil Aeronautics Authority, and later transferred to the Army Corps under Talley. The Civilian Conservation Corps, which had employed about 1,000 Alaska men, mostly in Southeast, before the war, moved into defense projects with communications and roads. Workers who built Annette Island airfield came from the CCC; so did some of the crews who helped build the naval air station at Sitka.

By Talley's figures, he eventually oversaw 28 of 39 wartime construction projects in Alaska.

In the early months of buildup, plans were to fortify Alaska's coast from Kodiak to Point Barrow, with forward air bases at McGrath and Nome, to protect against hostilities along Alaska's western coast. Rumors rampantly circulated that the Soviet Union and Germany planned a joint invasion of Alaska from Siberia. Then when Germany attacked Russia in June 1941, Japan became Alaska's bigger threat. Buckner shifted Alaska's defensive zone to the Aleutians.

This 1,200-mile island chain arcing through the North Pacific came within 650 miles of Japan's home islands. Buckner reasoned that Japan might target the Aleutians as a route into North America, and he also thought the islands would serve American forces well for possible attack on Japan's homeland. He authorized construction of defensive airfields at Cold Bay on the Alaska Peninsula and Otter Point on Umnak Island. He ordered them to be built in secret, with shipments to them addressed to bogus fish canneries, and requested that another staging field be built at Port Heiden.

Umnak's airfield would be the first-line defense of the Navy at Dutch Harbor. The field would remain secret long enough to surprise the unsuspecting Japanese.

A U.S. Fish and Wildlife raft approaches the rusting hull of a Japanese ship, most likely the Nozima Maru, a merchant ship, bombed at Kiska Harbor. In an operation dubbed "Cottage," the Allies sent about 35,000 men against an estimated 9,000 Japanese thought to occupy Kiska. In reality, the Japanese had a force of 6,000, about 700 of whom had been evacuated by submarines. The Allies were a little more than two weeks late with their invasion, though, because on July 28, the Japanese had ordered nine destroyers in under cover of fog to pick up the remaining men. (Edward Steele)

America At War: Pearl Harbor

On the morning of Dec. 7, 1941, Japan bombed the U.S. naval base at Pearl Harbor. The attack sunk or destroyed 19 ships and killed 2,300 people. The next day, the United States declared war on Japan, and three days later, war on Germany and Italy.

The military's communications system for the territory, formerly WAMCATS, was overworked and understaffed and had proven slow to respond. Perhaps not surprisingly, given its poor performance thus far,

news of Pearl Harbor came to Alaska's generals from a Fairbanks radio station, not the military. Broadcaster August Hiebert was getting ready to go on the air at KFAR radio station, tuning through the shortwave frequencies for news. And news he heard, a broadcast about the Pearl Harbor attack. He called commanders at Ladd Field, who notified Buckner in Anchorage.

Meanwhile, Alaska's Gov. Ernest Gruening in Juneau got a call from resident Tom Gardner, who'd heard about the attack on a Seattle radio station. Gruening checked with the Signal Corps, who'd heard

Artist Ogden Pleissner found himself assigned to Alaska as a war artist at the behest of Army Air Force Gen. Henry "Hap" Arnold. Commissioned as a captain, Pleissner was sent to the Aleutians, where he was to record in particular Army Air Force activities, producing paintings that Arnold planned to display in a museum the general hoped to establish after the war. In his diary, Pleissner wrote of the Aleutian weather: "Tried to paint outdoors today but the atmosphere is so damp that everything ran together." Pleissner still managed to produce sketches and watercolors including "Chow Line." (U.S. Army Art Collection, courtesy of The Center of Military History)

then were fired on; one was able to continue flying and landed safely. The other was never seen again. Bombers out of Cold Bay and Fort Glenn responded, and the Cold Bay group made contact.

One of those pilots, Capt. George Thornborough, unsuccessfully dropped his torpedo bombs on the carrier, then returned to Cold Bay to rearm. After he departed on his second sortie, he was never seen again. He was heard radioing Cold Bay toward dusk for help landing in the deteriorating weather. His wrecked plane was found about a month later on a beach about 90 miles from Cold Bay, where he'd crashed in a deadly miscalculation during his approach. The airfield at Cold Bay was named after him.

The evening of June 4, another group of fighters and bombers took off from the *Ryujo* and *Junyo* for a second-day's raid on Dutch. A bomb prematurely released by the enemy hit the village hospital in Unalaska, the Native community at the head of the bay from the naval base. The staff had just finished moving patients into dugout shelters so no one was hurt, although a nurse and janitor in the basement supply room were knocked down by the blast, which tore out the end of the building.

The sky filled with flack from anti-aircraft fire, as the planes turned to attack the ships. Plumes of water cascaded up as bombs plunged beneath the surface. One splintered the dock. Others hit ammunition magazines on the surrounding hillsides. Another exploded the dry-docked barracks ship *Northwestern* and flames spread to a warehouse in a fire that would last most of three days.

Photographs of the raid would later appear in *Life* magazine, comparing the attack on Dutch with that of Pearl Harbor. "Perhaps not so costly or deadly, but just as inexcusable," the magazine said.

In the two days of attack, American casualties at Dutch Harbor totaled 35 dead. Of those, 25 were new

arrivals to Fort Mears, who hadn't gotten orders to report to shelters and were killed in the first raid. Others killed included a civilian construction worker and four members of a seaplane crew on a mail run to Kodiak, whose plane was destroyed as it tried to take off. The 28 wounded included 25 of the newly arrived soldiers. In the air, 17 members of Army bomber crews and one fighter pilot were killed, and two men were wounded. On the Navy side, 23 men were killed, three were captured, 10 were declared missing in action and two were wounded, according to Cloe. Aircraft losses included two bombers, two fighters and six seaplanes.

The Japanese admitted to losing nine planes, including a Zero fighter later discovered in the

Military personnel, some still wearing World War I helmets, take cover during the first Japanese attack on Dutch Harbor, June 3, 1942. (Anchorage Museum)

two American fighter planes were downed. The group of P-40s, led by Col. Jack Chennault, was subsequently christened "The Aleutian Tigers," their airplane noses painted like striped bengals. The Umnak airbase was renamed Cape Field in honor of Lt. John Cape Jr., the only American pilot who died in the air fight.

Meanwhile in the western Aleutians, the Japanese task forces assigned to occupy Kiska and Attu moved into place; the attack and occupation of Adak had been canceled, and that force combined with the troops at Attu. The evening of June 6, about 1,200 enemy soldiers landed at Kiska. The next morning, they found the U.S. weather station and took nine Americans prisoner. The 10th weatherman evaded capture for 49 days until he finally surrendered, on the brink of starvation and exhaustion from exposure. They were shipped off to prisoner-of-war camp in Japan.

On June 7, another 1,200 enemy soldiers landed on Attu and captured the Native village. The white schoolteacher, Charles Foster Jones, started radioing Dutch for help as the Japanese came out of the hills behind the village. They rounded up the 42 villagers, questioned Jones and his wife, Etta, at length, then isolated the couple in a hut. Jones died as a result of the capture, although stories conflict as to how. The Japanese maintained that Jones committed suicide by slashing his wrist. The version told after the war by Mrs. Jones and the Attuans was that the Japanese soldiers shot Jones. The Attuans and Mrs. Jones were shipped to Kiska and then to Japan.

In the period of four days, World War II had spread to Alaska. While the Japanese had overwhelmingly failed to take Midway, suffering their first big defeat of the war, they bragged at home that they had occupied American soil. Alaska indeed seemed to be playing the role forecast years earlier by Mitchell and Dimond.

One of the most lamentable episodes of the war was the relocation of Alaska Natives from the Aleutians and Pribilofs to Southeast Alaska and the relocation and internment of Japanese living in Alaska to camps in the Lower 48. These Pribilof Islanders were evacuated from St. Paul and St. George islands in 1942. (National Archives, Photo No. 80-G-12163)

muskeg of Akutan Island. The plane was recovered by the Americans and taken to Dutch Harbor, where it was examined and shipped to the naval air station at San Diego and used for American training. Actor and later U.S. President Ronald Reagan even made a training film showing the characteristics of the Zero, using that plane.

Returning to their carriers after the June 4th bombing raid, the enemy planes flew directly over the still secret Umnak Island airfield and encountered some airborne American P-40s on patrol. As the planes flew at each other in battle, more P-40s took off to join in. In the ensuing dogfight, four enemy and dead in the water for a time, the Americans held back the enemy, which finally withdrew, erroneously thinking that American air planes were en route to do battle. This ended Japan's attempts to resupply by surface, leaving the job to submarines.

By now, the American commanders at headquarters in California were well into planning the retaking of Kiska and Attu, with Kiska targeted first. Air raids out of Amchitka and Adak intensified even more, despite periodic groundings from storms with 100-plus mph winds. In April alone, Kiska was attacked 83 times with 640 tons of bombs. Even so, the resilient Japanese seemed to be rebuilding as fast as they were being destroyed.

Because of a shortage of equipment and shipping, plans to retake the more heavily garrisoned Kiska were scrapped. Attu became the new objective, because it was thought to have only about 500 enemy soldiers. A division of Scouts would land in the dark, in advance of the main troops who would come shore in three locations, then converge on the enemy's main base at Chichagof Harbor. Artillery from ships and planes would cover the ground troops.

The 7th Infantry Division, in training for desert combat in North Africa, was reassigned to the Attu landing. They were given a few weeks of amphibious training off San Clemente Island, but their mission remained secret; medical officers continued lecturing about tropical diseases. When they were finally aboard transports headed north, they learned their destination. They rendezvoused in Dutch Harbor with other troops coming from Cold Bay. All totaled, about 10,000 men, three battleships, six cruisers, 19 destroyers, two submarines and dozens of auxiliary vessels assembled, the largest American force since the Battle of North Africa, the previous November.

Bad weather delayed the Attu landing until May 11, 1943. Despite impenetrable fog, the troops went

ashore. The fog was so bad, in fact, that two ships collided, putting both out of service. The first American casualties were four soldiers drowned when a transport dropped its ramp before hitting the beach, filled with water and sank. But by that evening, the first round of American soldiers, about 3,500, were on Attu.

By the next morning, it was clear that the three-day mission was going to take much longer. The troops made slow progress inland, with their trucks and tractors bogging down in the mud. The enemy fired down from upland positions; they had been expecting an invasion sometime in May, having intercepted American intelligence.

The fog made American air support and naval gunfire difficult if not impossible. Enemy submarines fired torpedoes at American ships, which were still

Landing craft come ashore during the Battle of Attu, May 1943. (U.S. Government photo, courtesy of Jack Haugen)

Supplies are brought ashore during the Attu invasion. (U.S. Government photo, courtesy of Jack Haugen)

unloading troops and supplies. By May 15, American commanders were demanding more troops and road building equipment; the Attu garrison was judged by now to be at least 2,500 Japanese.

Gradually, the Attu occupation force began to gain ground, aided by air attacks from fighters and bombers as the weather lifted. The Japanese were running low on rations and requested reinforcements had not arrived. On the seventh day, the southern and northern landing forces met. The enemy stubbornly retreated to several steep, narrow passes, where heavy fighting continued amid snow and fog. On one ridge, the Japanese were killed in their fox holes in a daring ascent led by a single soldier through enemy machine-gun fire. Hand-to-hand fighting with grenades, bayonets and rifle butts characterized the enemy's resistance as the Americans pushed through, bearing down on Chichagof Harbor.

By the morning of May 29, the Japanese were encircled by American troops. Believing that death was more honorable than capture, the Japanese commander ordered all injured killed with injections of morphine. His remaining men, about 1,000 of them, charged up the valley in a suicidal counterattack. They ran, firing their way through two American command posts and a medical detachment, continuing toward a pass at the head of the valley, cutting telephone wires as they went. But on Engineer Hill, the advancing Japanese were stopped by gunfire from a hastily organized American defensive line. They attacked repeatedly, until the remaining few Japanese soldiers blew themselves up with grenades. By evening, the slopes of Engineer Hill were littered with combat carnage.

In the days that followed, the Americans hunted down the remaining Japanese and buried the dead. About 2,350 Japanese soldiers died on Attu; only 29 were taken prisoner. The battle claimed 549 American lives, some of them killed by friendly fire in the bombing raids. Another 1,148 Americans were wounded, and another 2,100 were taken out of action, according to Cloe, from accidents, disease, exhaustion and being inadequately clothed for the cold, wet weather.

Attu was one of the most costly assaults in the Pacific, according to an Army history, second only to the taking of Iwo Jima, which occurred in early 1945.

Now Kiska remained.

The Army engineers quickly constructed a new airfield on Attu, at Alexai Point, and one on Shemya Island to launch bombers and fighters against Kiska. Surface and air attacks continued to weaken enemy forces in preparation for an August invasion.

The air base on Attu also gave American fliers another target. On July 10, a bombing raid against Japanese installations in the northern Kuriles took off from Attu, the first land-based attack against the Japanese home islands. That same day, seaplanes from Adak and Attu flew a mission over the Kuriles. Several more raids followed, to bomb the ports and take aerial photographs.

In *Home from Siberia* (1990), Otis Hays Jr. tells the account of 291 airmen from the Aleutian bases who were forced to divert to the Soviet Union during these strikes, and were held captive until after the war.

In the meantime, unbeknownst to U.S. commanders, the Japanese were preparing to abandon Kiska. They started evacuating Kiska by submarine, a tediously slow process. Finally the Japanese commanders assembled a fleet of ships to sail in under fog cover and remove the remaining troops.

All the while, American bombers continued their raids, intermittently because of the weather, through June and July. On the evening of July 23, an American seaplane on patrol made radar contact with what appeared to be seven vessels about 200 miles southwest of Attu. The Navy ordered a task force, including two ships guarding the harbor entrance at Kiska, to intercept the vessels, assumed to be Japanese resupply ships. The American ships sailed toward the target, now appearing on radar about 90 miles southwest of Kiska. When within range, eight to 12 miles away, they started firing. The radar blips disappeared one by one. A search of the area the next morning failed to reveal any wreckage, however, and the incident was attributed to a radar anomaly caused by unusual atmospheric conditions.

Another theory of what caused the "Battle of the Pips," as it came to be known, was presented in 1993 during the Alaska at War Symposium. During his keynote address, author Brian Garfield told of hearing from Aleutian fishing captain George Fulton, who'd read Garfield's book *The Thousand-Mile War: World War II in Alaska and the Aleutians* (1982). Fulton theorized that the Navy's radar had detected huge flocks of shearwaters. These migratory waterbirds feed in the Aleutians during the summer.

They can be detected on radar when they congregate in the air by the hundreds of thousands, zigzagging across the water. Then as they land on the water to feed, they disappear from radar. Fishermen today, wrote Fulton, rely on radar to avoid sailing into the flocks, which litter their decks, but signals from the birds can also be useful, leading fishermen to plankton beds where pollock feed.

In any event back in 1943, while the U.S. Navy ships were off battling the pips and then stopping for an evening to refuel, the Japanese fleet sailed into Kiska Harbor and rescued their troops. It was an amazingly efficient operation. Enemy radar had found an opening in the American blockade, created by the departed ships, and broke radio silence with a terse code, signaling the troops to assemble. The men were waiting on the beach when the ships arrived, and they quickly boarded 39 landing craft. Within 55 minutes, all 5,183 men were aboard six destroyers and two cruisers, and the ships were on their way home. The Japanese had given up the Aleutians.

In the days to come, as bombing intensified, some Americans began to suspect Kiska was empty.

Aerial photographs showed the same scenes day

After the attacks of June 1942, the war moved past Dutch Harbor into the western Aleutians. Personnel at Dutch had time for more light-hearted pursuits, such as this Carmen Miranda act performed during a Navy show at Fort Mears in the fall 1943. (National Archives, courtesy of the National Park Service, Alaska Region)

after day, with no repairs made to bomb-damaged buildings, no movement of trucks and barges. Radio communications had ceased. Four fighter pilots, after performing low-altitude maneuvers over the main airfield without drawing enemy fire, even landed and got out of their planes to investigate, writes Cloe. They returned with news of the Japanese exodus, but were reprimanded for their reckless actions. Gen. Butler was convinced that the Japanese were gone, but Adm. Kinkaid, now in charge of the Navy, thought the enemy had retreated to the hills, as they had done on Attu. He thought the invasion

would be good practice for the troops.

The landing force consisted of about 30,000 Americans and 5,300 Canadians. Three battleships, two cruisers, 19 destroyers and 70 other assorted Navy vessels were allotted to the invasion. Air power rested in 24 heavy bombers, 44 medium bombers, 28 dive bombers, 60 fighters and 12 patrol bombers. As on Attu, the Scouts would land first.

On Aug. 15, with warships targeting the main enemy gun positions on the south and east, troops started coming ashore on the north and west sides of the island. A special force of Canadian and American soldiers trained in winter mountaineering and back-country travel came ashore first, along with the Scouts. What was to be a quick, smoothly executed night landing turned into eight confusing hours as the troop transports stacked up offshore, battling the cold, choppy surf for a place to go in. The only gunfire the soldiers encountered came from each other, shooting through the fog at movements thought to be the enemy, in what later was dubbed the "optical Aleutian."

Accidental encounters like this killed 17 Americans and four Canadians, writes Cloe. Booby traps rigged by the enemy also claimed some lives. Seventy-one men died and 47 were wounded when a destroyer hit a Japanese mine offshore. Within a few days, as troops combed the island and found uneaten meals on tables, games abandoned in play, piles of supplies and equipment, it was clear that the Japanese had left in a hurry. A few dogs were the only living traces of the Japanese occupation; one of the dogs had lived at the Kiska weather station before the Japanese arrived.

Looking Back

With the exception of the Battle of the Komandorskis and the assault on Attu, the Aleutian campaign consisted primarily of seizing mostly

Two Navy Seabees (right) share their lunch with ski troopers from the Army's 7th Division during the battle for Attu in May 1943. (U.S. Government photo, courtesy of Jack Haugen)

In July 1942, the Western Defense Command, in charge of protecting Alaska, ordered the Alaska Barge Terminal built on Excursion Inlet, east of Glacier Bay in Southeastern Alaska. The $18 million terminal was completed in November 1943; earlier that same year, however, the Japanese threat to shipping in the eastern Gulf of Alaska had been removed and the terminal became superfluous. By 1945, as the war was winding down, the military pondered the fate of the huge base in the Alaska wilderness. Deciding that some of the construction costs could be recouped by salvaging construction materials from the project, the military had the Army bring in 700 German prisoners of war to tear down the facility. This photo shows three POWs at work in the shoe repair shop within the stockade. (U.S. Army Signal Corps, Photo No. PCA 175-118)

unoccupied islands by both sides, and the bombing of enemy positions by American forces.

According to historian Cloe's figures, the American-Canadian force grew to 144,000 by the eve of the Kiska invasion; the Japanese at their peak had only about 8,500 soldiers in the Aleutians. U.S. air power in Alaska during this time grew from 4,489 personnel, when Dutch was attacked, to 16,526 with the landing on Kiska. About 1,000 men died or were declared missing in action during the Aleutian campaign. Of the 225 U.S. Army, Navy and RCAF airplanes that were disabled, only 41 were destroyed in combat. Most of the others were lost due to accidents, most of which were weather-related.

Even during an invasion laundry has to be attended to. This 7th Division trooper checks out the facilities at Holtz Bay, Attu, in May 1943. (U.S. Government photo, courtesy of Jack Haugen)

The Japanese suffered the loss of most all their men on Attu and about 500 on Kiska before the evacuation, along with about 1,000 men at sea and 150 airmen, according to Cloe.

"In the final analysis," he concludes, "the Aleutians should have been left to the Aleuts. The troops employed there could have been put to better use elsewhere and the billions of dollars hastily spent to build and sustain a military infrastructure on the islands used more wisely in other theaters.

"In the end, the price of pride was paid for by the young men, American, Canadian and Japanese, who fought with great bravery and then were forgotten by history."

The Rest of the War

With the Japanese no longer a threat in the Aleutians, the Pacific commanders generally lost interest in Alaska. By late 1944, they were pulling troops out of the territory and closing down bases. Still, more people than ever before lived in Alaska; its population swelled some 40 percent, to more than 100,000 people, from prewar levels. Anchorage, the Army's headquarters during the war, was now the largest city in Alaska, with Fairbanks about to overtake Juneau in size.

Despite its drawdown, the military maintained its presence in the western Aleutians and in Anchorage and Fairbanks. At these bases and a few other locations, military assignments continued through the final months of war.

Construction continued on the CANOL pipeline in Canada, even though the war in Alaska, for all practical purposes, was over. A refinery started processing 3,000 barrels a day into aviation fuel, gasoline and motor oil in April 1944 and operated until the Army closed the line in June 1945. The project had cost $138 million.

Some of the more noteable activities that took place out of Fairbanks and Cold Bay toward the end of the war were associated with America's Lend-Lease program. This program had been enacted in March 1941 as a way to assist Britain against Germany by supplying guns, ships and ammunition. After Germany invaded Russia, the Lend-Lease provisions were extended to provide aid to the Soviet Union.

American pilots flew Lend-Lease aircraft up through Canada along the staging route to Ladd Field in Fairbanks, Alaska's central staging area for the transfers. The Soviets maintained a large contingent of pilots, mechanics and other military personnel there. They were given their own section of the base, but their officers shared many privileges with the American officers. The Soviets frequently shopped in town, buying candy, perfume, lingerie, canned goods and other items to take home, crammed into empty corners of the aircrafts. After a brief training stint, the Soviet pilots would fly the planes on to Siberia, through military checkpoints in Galena and Nome. The route became an unofficial shortcut for dignitaries traveling between the two countries and likely served as an espionage channel for military secrets.

The transfer of planes started in September 1942. More than 7,900 airplanes flew through Fairbanks along this route to Siberia during the war. Planes also were transferred to Russia via South America and Africa, and by sea transport, but by far the majority came through Alaska. The Lend-Lease program helped Russia withstand enemy sieges of Stalingrad and Leningrad and eventually drive the German troops from eastern Europe.

Another, lesser known part of the Lend-Lease program was accomplished through Cold Bay on the Alaska Peninsula. The Yalta Conference in February 1945 brought Russia into the war against Japan. Transfers of American ships to Russia commenced out of Cold Bay, with Soviet sailors trained there in secret, a mission called Operation HULA. For six months in 1945, men of the Soviet Navy worked alongside American sailors, preparing for Russia's amphibious assault on Japanese bases in the Kuriles. Some of the landing crafts and crews trained at Cold Bay led the Russian attack against Paramushiro in the Kuriles; others participated in operations against Japanese positions in North Korea and on Sakhalin Island, according to naval historian Richard Russell. By September 1945 when the program ended, 149 vessels had been transferred and 12,400 Russian sailors trained at Cold Bay.

Meanwhile, American bombing raids on the Japanese-held Kuriles had continued out of bases on Adak, Shemya and Attu. The last mission over the Kuriles from Alaska was flown on Sept. 3, 1945, to gather intelligence on the Soviets, who had just occupied the islands, according to Cloe. Soviet fighters turned back the American fliers, a prelude of the tensions that would characterize the coming Cold War.

The action in the Kuriles was some of the last of World War II. The battles in Europe culminated in Hitler's surrender on May 7, 1945, after Allied troops stormed Germany. Bombing raids through June wore down Japanese defenses, and on Aug. 6 and 9, U.S. planes dropped atomic bombs on Hiroshima and Nagasaki. Japan surrendered on Aug. 14, 1945.

After the war, 24 Aleut survivors were returned and resettled in Atka, because their village on Attu had been destroyed. About 90 Aleut men were taken to the Pribilofs in 1943 to harvest seals; the rest of the Aleut refugees interned in Southeast were returned to the Aleutians after the war. They found their homes and churches vandalized. The villages of Biorka, Makushin and Kashega were never resettled. In 1989,

A U.S. submarine returns from a Pacific patrol to a welcoming crowd at Dutch Harbor. (Archives, University of Alaska Fairbanks, Hanna Call Collection, Photo No. 70-11-27N)

RIGHT:
Before evacuating Kiska, the Japanese destroyed these midget submarines that they had hidden in an island trench. (U.S. Government photo, courtesy of Jack Haugen)

BELOW:
A group of SPARS, female Coast Guard personnel, leave the front entrance of the Federal Building in Ketchikan on June 17, 1945. With its island-studded coast and miles of shoreline, Southeast depended heavily on the Coast Guard to protect its waterways. (Courtesy of Tongass Historical Society, Photo No. 95.2.81)

the Aleuts received $27 million in reparation payments, including money for church restorations, as part of a larger package that included the Japanese-Americans interned during the war.

National Historical Landmarks

In recent years, efforts to recognize World War II history in Alaska have resulted in eight war sites being designated as National Historic Landmarks. This is the highest level of official recognition accorded to sites of historical significance.

They are Kodiak Naval Operating Base and Forts Greely and Abercrombie, Kodiak Island; Sitka Naval Operating Base and U.S. Army Coastal Defenses, Sitka; Adak Army Base and Adak Naval Operating Base, Adak Island; Attu Battlefield and U.S. Army and Navy Airfields, Attu Island; Cape Field at Fort Glenn, Umnak Island; Dutch Harbor Naval Operating Base and Fort Mears U.S. Army, Unalaska Island; Japanese Occupation Site, Kiska Island; and Ladd Field (Fort Wainwright), Fairbanks.

In addition, a B-24 Liberator on Atka Island is listed on the National Register of Historic Places. Marks Field at Nome and the railroad spur to Whittier were nominated for the National Register, but not accepted.

Caines Head State Recreation Area in Seward, another historic World War II site, is in the process of being nominated to the National Register. This state park includes Fort McGilvray and coastal defense sites around Resurrection Bay. Visitors to the park today can hike two miles from the North Beach landing to the fort with its well-preserved concrete bunker, can fish off an old Army dock at North Beach, or explore an abundance of wartime relics on South Beach where most of the activity took place. Jack Turnbull, who served at Caines Head during the war, now lives in Seward and helps take care of the park. He has made important contributions in helping interpret its history, says Jack Sinclair, Kenai District ranger who served as the Caines Head ranger until funding for the position was cut.

The movement to recognize Alaska's World War II sites gained momentum in the late 1970s, when the National Park Service started gathering information about war sites associated with the Pacific campaign. A few in Alaska, such as the Kodiak naval base, already were on the National Register but hadn't achieve landmark status. The park service, with architects from its historical architecture records division, mapped, photographed and further documented sites, particularly those involved in the Aleutian campaign.

About this same time, the U.S. Army Corps of Engineers started a program to clean up old defense sites in Alaska under legislation passed in 1983. In the beginning, the program focused on the Aleutian sites. Cleanup included disposing of hazardous materials, unexploded ordnance and old buildings at World War II sites.

In 1986 and 1987, the secretary of Interior designated the five sites in the Aleutian Islands as National Historic Landmarks. Still today, much work remains to be done in documenting and interpreting these sites.

At times, the two agencies have targeted the same war relics with different interpretations about what should be done. Most problematic has been reconciling the definition of "historic." For instance, war-era buildings on Unalaska Island and a bridge on Attu were targeted for removal by the Army corps, yet were considered by the park service to be important to the historic integrity and cultural interpretation of the sites. A joint task force formed by the agencies tried to resolve such differences.

In 1990, the Army Corps identified and inventoried every defense site in Alaska, a total of about 700 that includes post-World War II and active sites, to prioritize sites where remediation is needed. About 250 defense sites in Alaska are listed for further cleanup. In the meantime, what started as a general cleanup program for Alaska sites has evolved into a nationwide program of defense site cleanups, targeting hazardous and toxic wastes. Alaska gets only a share of the funding, in competition with other states. All sites picked for cleanup are subject to

Civilians actively participated in the defense of Alaska. In this simulated defense of Ketchikan by the 297th Infantry, National Guard, Company B, gunner Bob Wikstrom and assistant gunner Pat Hagiwara man the machine gun, while Tommy Davies (fourth in line) and Joe Friedman look out. The man with the cigarette is unidentified. (Bill Lattin, courtesy of the Tongass Historical Society, Photo No. 88.1.6138)

Dear Editor:

I was based at Cold Bay for two years. In January 1942, we docked at King Cove, one company of infantry, two companies of engineers. Then we went to Cold Bay on barges and fishing boats, losing much equipment, barges sinking. We waded ashore and set up tents. We were advance units of the 35th division. Cold Bay was uninhabited.

The log building is our Recreation Hall and Theater built in 1942 by Army engineers. The logs were floated in. A boom was rigged using timbers, ropes and pulleys to hoist the logs in place. Two log buildings were built, one for officers, one for enlisted men. We had one U.S.O. show. I do not remember names, but to us they were all headline stars.

The quarters at our camp at Cold Bay were for the most part pre-fab, of wood, called K.D.s for "knock down," designed for six men, made do for nine. We were just off the beach. The sand was at least 10 feet deep. Any farther away would be muskeg, and that is a no no, as we found out the first night. Tent poles sink.

The Intelligence and Reconnaissance Section maintained outposts. Amak Island north of Cold Bay was one of them. The trip from Cold Bay to Amak was two days. In rough weather, longer, with an overnight stop at False Pass, an American cannery and dock. A 10-man squad

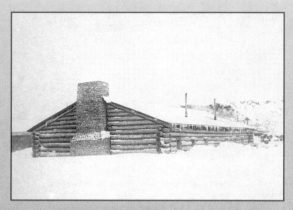

CLOCKWISE, FROM LEFT:
■ *A member of the USO points to the sign at the general store in King Cove in 1943.* ■ *One of two log buildings built by Army engineers at Cold Bay in 1943.* ■ *Cpl. Iuka and Harold Schubert work on the dugout built by the crew on Amak Island in 1943.* ■ *Pre-fab construction characterizes the camp at Cold Bay in 1943. (Photos courtesy of William Weaver)*

was stationed at Amak, usually for about six weeks a tour. My last tour was close to three months, due to bad weather. Six Alaska Scouts, working in pairs, manned an outpost on the far side of the island. We had a phone line for communication to base, three radio operators to contact the mainland, and one man from the weather squadron for reports. The sea lions would gather near our outpost. Amak is just a mountain sticking up in the Bering Sea. Snow was on the peak all year. Each man would prepare meals for one day. Supplies were brought with each crew; some supplies and mail were dropped from aircraft.

We found that our area of Amak had been used as a hunting camp, probably many times. It was very old with many walrus skulls and tusks. Cpl. Iuka, our leader, was very inventive and started some of us carving ivory. This led to more excavations and we found evidence of dug-out dwellings. We found some crude tools, mostly spoons hacked out of ivory, an old ship's lantern, an odd-shaped ax and some Russian cartridge cases of brass. This prompted us to duplicate the Native dugout. The walls and roof were lined with wood from the beach and mounded over with earth from the hole. We also dug a well for fresh water.

—William Weaver
St. Ann, Mo.

The Japanese left behind all manner of equipment and supplies when they evacuated Kiska Island in late July 1943. (U.S. Government photo, courtesy of Jack Haugen)

periods of comment and review by the public and other government agencies.

In another development on Unalaska Island, the Aleut village Ounalashka Corp. is trying to have World War II sites there designated as a national park and has been lobbying Congress for enabling legislation. The corporation owns most of Unalaska Island and would retain ownership of any land included in a national park. Private ownership of national parks, which has been successfully accomplished already in several cases, is considered the trend of the future as

government funding of park lands purchases decreases. A national park created around the Unalaska war sites would include an interpretative center, displays and other elements of interest to tourists and visitors.

It is through these efforts — preserving a visual history of the war on the landscape, interpreting wartime events and actions, and honoring the individuals and groups of people involved — that Alaska's World War II sacrifices and contributions will be more fully recognized. ■

A "Western Union Boy" in the Aleutians

By Murray Morgan

Editor's note: *A book review columnist for* The News Tribune *in Tacoma, Wash., Murray Morgan is an author and historian whose wrote his first book,* Bridge to Russia *(1947), about the Aleutian chain.*

My war with the Aleutians began long after the fighting ended. The last Japanese on Attu had been killed and those on Kiska had fled nearly a year before our troopship left Seattle for a "destination unspecified." Nine days later, on May 4, 1944, we entered the harbor at Adak. The sun was shining. The blue water of the Bering Sea lapped against a shore cluttered with warehouses, Quonset huts and tents. Beyond the man-made mess, slopes of deep green tundra rose to the base of a 4,000-foot volcano, its rust-colored ridges veiled angel-white with snow. We had not expected beauty and it did not last. Before we could disembark and disperse to our assigned stations, Mount Moffett disappeared behind fast-forming clouds, not to be seen again for days. We had been given Aleutian basic training lesson no. 1: Weather changes fast, especially if it's good.

I had been sent north as a cryptographic technician (private first class) with the Alaska Communication System, an anomalous adjunct to the Army Signal Corps. Originally called the Washington Alaska Military Cable and Telegraph System, WAMCATS was created in 1904 to provide dot-dash telegraph service among Alaska communities and to establish an electronic link between Alaska and the rest of the country. Handling civilian messages as well as military kept the ACS in contact with the public. It developed a distinctly un-GI personality. "Real Soldiers" on the chain looked on us as Western Union boys pretending to be warriors. Even worse, we in the ACS could count on being rotated back to the mainland after a year in isolation. Other troops had to mark off 730 days on their calendars before they could hope to get out. But for all of us the war had become sitzkrieg not blitzkrieg, a matter of sitting it out.

As a cryptographer, which really meant code clerk, my assignment was to spend eight hours a day in a windowless room behind double-locked doors typing on a SIGABA, a secret electronic device that automatically turned English into code or returned code to English. This required about as much intelligence as working a crossword puzzle but we were pleased to let our hut-mates think we might be struggling to decipher Japanese codes. We liked to be called "signal intelligence."

My year took me to three islands, Adak, Umnak, and Attu, which is so far west that the international dateline has been bent to keep it in the same day as the rest of America. New Zealand, which is directly south of Attu, has Monday while Attu is having Sunday.

ACS stations in the Aleutians tended to be similar in layout, different in personality. The transmitter was usually on a hillside, well away from the main base. The central buildings were: headquarters, mess hall and supply shack, with a random scattering of Pacific huts nestled in the tundra to prevent their being blown away in storms. The huts were variously described as prefabricated igloos or short tunnels. Walls were curved, which tended to distort the inevitable pin-ups. Furnishings consisted of from eight to 10 cots, and an oil stove in the middle of the room. There was no running water and latrines always seemed to be more than a block away, a considerable distance in a williwaw. You learned to keep your parka buttoned tight whenever you went out lest a gust get through a crack, balloon the rain gear and send the wearer spinning off the ever-damp boardwalks into snow stained yellow by those who couldn't wait.

At each post the basic gripes were about the total absence of women and trees and the unending proximity of our fellow men. Differences were inevitable among small groups confined to bleak quarters for prolonged periods. Many of the quarrels involved the volume of the radio. Duty hours varied. One man's sack time was another's rec time, and even those on the same shift might differ in taste. On Attu, our hut-leader, Gene Elliott, in civilian life an authority on 19th-century British music halls, put it this way:

Oh, poets sing of the silent north
And little do they know!
For it's plain to see that they weren't around
In the days of the radio.

A bunch of the boys were whooping it up
On the local NBC,
And it may send you and it may send him
But it doesn't do much for me.

I'll walk alone in the frozen wastes
And try to commune with God,
Singing cow-cow boogie the strangest way
And nobody thinks its odd.

Don't Fence Me In with The Trolley Song
At the End of a Perfect Day.
I Dream of More Than You Dream I Do.
My Buddy. Going My Way?

Whatever the hardship, we survived. I was rotated out 370 days after arrival. Looking down from the DC3 flying me to Anchorage, I thought Mount Moffett even more beautiful than at first sight. ∎

LEFT:
Murray Morgan (right) fights what he describes as the "Battle of Umnak" in December 1944. (Courtesy of Murray Morgan)

LOWER LEFT:
Author of several history books, Murray Morgan spent part of World War II in the Aleutians decoding Japanese communiqués. Several of the military personnel assigned to Alaska during World War II had become well-known or would become well-known in civilian life, in literature, art, music and film. Gore Vidal served as first mate aboard an Army ship transporting men and supplies in the Aleutians. Dashiell Hammett, author of The Maltese Falcon *and other mysteries, was editor of* The Adakian, *the rag from Adak. Bernard Kalb, later an NBC newsman, joined Hammett on the paper. The director of the movie "The Maltese Falcon," John Huston, was sent to the Aleutians with the Army Signal Corps to record the birth of the Adak base and the bombing attacks against the then-Japanese-held islands of Attu and Kiska. His efforts produced the documentary "Report From the Aleutians," the first of three films he made about Allied activities during World War II. As it turned out, "Report From the Aleutians" was the only full-length film made about the war in Alaska. (Mary Randlett, courtesy of Murray Morgan)*

Reflections of Army Life at Kodiak

By Charles Gum

Editor's note: *Charles Gum lives in West Virginia, and visits Kodiak occasionally, recalling his time on Kodiak more than 50 years ago for members of the Kodiak Historical Society.*

The 201st Infantry Regiment was the West Virginia National Guard Unit. It was activated into federal service Jan. 6, 1941. In April, new draftee recruits were sent to the 201st for basic training. That was when I was inducted.

I was in the Antitank Co. of the 201st. Only part of the regiment went to Kodiak at first. One battalion was sent to Sitka in Southeastern Alaska. One battalion, plus headquarters and at least parts of Service Co., Medical Co. and Antitank Co. were sent to Kodiak.

As part of that first group, I was with a detachment that arrived at Kodiak, Sept. 16, 1941, on a World War I Liberty ship, the *St. Mihiel*, refitted as a troop carrier. When we arrived at Kodiak, the tent city area was somewhat prepared. Some tents were already occupied. Some were completed, others only the frame was up and the tent had to be placed over the frame and laced up. In most cases the vertical part of the tent frame was covered with boards around the sides, to about 4 feet high.

The tents were arranged in double rows, back to back, with the backs of the tents only 2 or 3 feet apart. The front of the tents faced a fairly wide street or space. Doorways were sometimes added in the entrance of the tents, depending on available materials and the ingenuity of the occupants.

The tents were square, had wooden floors, and in the center was a wooden frame in which there was gravel or sand on which a Sibley stove stood. The stove was somewhat like an inverted funnel, with a pipe running out the top of the tent. There was a metal cap at the top of the tent to cover the opening, and through which the pipe extended.

These tents, known as pyramidal tents, could house six people, though that varied. In our case, a squad tent as we called it, had five people with two double-deck bunks, and a single bunk for the squad leader.

Tent City was located on a flat area, south and a little east of the low hills at the foot of Barometer Mountain. The Kodiak-to-Navy-Base road went around the south side of the main part of Tent City, however, some tents were on the south side of the road, where officers' living quarters and Regimental Headquarters were located. The military airport was built generally between Tent City and the beach, near the main entrance to the harbor.

At first we scavenged any wood, or driftwood, that we could find to fuel our stoves when the weather began to get cold. Later, ships brought in supplies, including sacks of coal briquettes, and presto logs. For quite a while during fall and early winter of 1941 much of the work to unload the ships was done by G.I.s. We worked shifts of four hours, then had eight hours off. Sometimes instead of working at the ship, we would work at the warehouse, unloading supplies from trucks and storing them in the warehouse. As I remember, the hardest work was moving large sacks of coal. This seemed like a hectic schedule because the eight hours off included travel time, meals, sleep and other incidentals.

We, the Antitank Co., lived in Tent City from arrival in August 1941 to May 1942. Conditions improved somewhat during that time. A recreation room, a frame building, was located at the back end of the Company row of tents. It was in use by Christmas 1941. In fact, we had a rather peaceful Christmas party. A pool table was provided.

A makeshift building was put up at the back of the Company area and was fitted for a laundry room, with an electric washer. Water had to be heated over a fire. One man from the Company was assigned to operate the laundry.

We also had a night watchman for the Company. One person was given that job and was excused from other regular duties. He was to watch for anything unusual, for fire, and also was to keep fires going in certain tents.

For some time after arrival in Kodiak, the Antitank Co. did not have a kitchen of its own. Instead, we got our meals with the Alabama Engineering Co., which lived in the row of tents next to us. In time, our kitchen and dining building, generally known as the mess hall, was constructed at the front end of the Company area, near the road.

Life in Tent City before Dec. 7, 1941, was less restricted than it became after the war started. Weekends were mostly free of duty. We could relax, catch up on correspondence or explore the area. Climbing to the top of Barometer Mountain was a challenge that many tried.

With war time came blackout regulations, preparation of defense positions for our 37mm Antitank guns, more strict guard duty. Work went on regardless of weather.

In this second part of the continuing story of my time at Kodiak, I have concentrated on the Sunday services and related happenings.

As part of the military program, chaplains are provided to see to the religious services and to counsel as needed. One chaplain, Maj. William Cline, came to Kodiak in 1941 along with the 201st Infantry Regimental Headquarters and the first battalion group.

I don't recall how soon Sunday services were held, but I'm sure it was not long after arrival. A large tent was erected near the main road. The only musical instrument was a small portable organ that folded up to look like a large suitcase.

The one service in the big tent that stands out in memory was on Dec. 7, 1941. During the service, there occurred the unusual sound of a bugle call. Immediately the officers attending service got up and left. An hour or two after services ended, we learned Pearl Harbor had been attacked and we were at war.

After the war declaration, our Sundays were no longer free of duty. But the chaplain depended on me to play the organ. As it turned out, the chaplain would call my Company Commander and ask for my help. If I was out at a guard post or other duty, a Company truck would be sent out to bring me in for the service. My Company Commander then was Capt. James Robison, who always cooperated with the chaplain.

When in May 1942 the 201st Infantry moved from Tent City to the new barracks area, our Sunday services were then held in the new Faith Chapel.

Chaplain Cline, with the rank of major, was the chief chaplain at Kodiak. He was a Lutheran by denomination, but as a Protestant chaplain, his services were non-denominational to serve all. A new Catholic chaplain, Chaplain Gordon, came to Faith Chapel late in 1942. Chaplain Cline and Chaplain Gordon each had an office at Faith Chapel. I remember meeting Chaplain Gordon only once, a few days before I left Kodiak. My last Sunday at Kodiak and at Faith Chapel was Nov. 29, 1942. The new organist for Faith Chapel was Cpl. Nelson Boone, also of Antitank Co. ∎

Charles Gum and his fellow troopers from the 201st Infantry Regiment lived at Tent City, located near the base of Barometer Mountain between downtown Kodiak and the current Coast Guard facility, from August 1941 to May 1942. (Sgt. Clevenger Collection, courtesy of the Kodiak Historical Society)

The Quonset Hut in Alaska

By D. Colt Denfeld, Ph.D.

Editor's note: *Dr. Denfeld is a historian for the Alaska District, Army Corps of Engineers, who for the past 20 years has been investigating the history of military posts in Alaska. Dr. Denfeld estimates there were 20,000 to 30,000 Quonset huts in Alaska by the end of World War II. In addition to the Quonset and Pacific huts discussed in this article, Dr. Denfeld points out that there was a third hut, seldom used in Alaska, the Jamesway. This shelter, similar in appearance to the Quonset, was wood-ribbed with a rubberized canvas covering, about the same size as a Quonset, and functioned primarily as very temporary shelter.*

The Quonset hut exemplifies American technological ingenuity and problem solving. It was an efficient design, created in record time and built in record numbers.

As war clouds darkened in March 1941, Adm. Ben Moreell, chief of the Navy's Yards and Docks, wondered how he would shelter troops at the planned advance bases. He discussed his concerns with the George A. Fuller Co., a contractor with experience in base construction. Moreell wanted a hut that provided the most protection and comfort at the lowest cost. This hut had to be prefabricated and of knockdown design, built in the United States and shipped to distant bases. It also had to be easily and quickly assembled by troops in the field.

On March 30, Moreell gave the Fuller Co. the go-ahead to create and build a first installment of huts. If successful, their design would be manufactured by a number of steelworks. The admiral expected and demanded an unbelievable schedule, the first batch of huts was to be ready for shipment in 60 days, on June 1.

Fuller Co. dove into the project, trying designs and building test models. The design team studied the British Nissen hut, a semicylindrical steel hut, named for its creator, Captain Nissen. Analysis of the Nissen found it inadequate, it had too many elaborate parts and required skilled workers to assemble. However, Fuller stayed with the steel, semicylindrical design.

The simpler Fuller product was a half-circle, corrugated steel structure on arch ribs, with insulation between the steel exterior and a pressed-wood interior wall. It could be placed on a concrete foundation, pilings, or on the ground with a wood floor. The ends, or bulkheads, were wood with a door and two windows. Initially the housing and office units were 16 feet by 36 feet, but were replaced by 20-foot by 40-foot and 20-foot by 56-foot units. The larger units allowed for an overhang at the ends for shade in the tropics and increased space in the cold regions to accommodate the occupants' extra clothing, gear and a heater. There was also a 40-foot by 100-foot warehouse unit and other versions. Designed at Fuller's Quonset Point, Rhode Island facility, the hut was named a Quonset.

The Army recognized the Quonset hut as ideal for its forward bases. Following the attack on Pearl Harbor, and the tremendous military buildup in Alaska, the Army Corps of Engineers ordered 16,000 Quonsets for bases here. Shipments were made in December, sending Quonsets to the secret bases at Umnak Island and Cold Bay. The packing crates bound for Cold Bay bore the name Saxton and Co., a fictitious fishing firm. Those headed to Umnak Island were marked Blair Packing Co. The ruse worked. When the Japanese attacked Dutch Harbor on June 3, 1942, they were completely unaware of the airbase at nearby Umnak. Quonsets were also erected at Annette Island, Yakutat, Nome, Cordova, Juneau, Port Heiden, Adak, Amchitka, Attu, Kiska, Shemya and many small bases.

The Quonset hut was ideal for Alaska, allowing

NAME / LOCATION / DESCRIPTION:	CONSTRUCTION:*	SERVED HERE:	AFTER THE WAR:

■ **DUTCH HARBOR NAVAL OPERATING BASE / FORT MEARS** (Dutch Harbor and Fort Mears NHL)
Unalaska and Amaknak islands
    Naval section base established Jan. 1941; naval air station added June 1941; bombed by Japanese, June 3 and 4, 1942; designated naval operating base July 1942; included air station, submarine base, Marine barracks, radio station, section base, Akutan refueling depot, other naval shore activities.
    Fort Mears was Army headquarters to defend naval base; included Mount Ballyhoo and Unalaska garrisons, Hog Island and Summer Bay cantonments, and fixed harbor defenses at Eider Point, Ulakta Head, Hill 400 and Summer Bay; search lights and observation posts at Constantine Head, Erskine Point, Cape Wislow and Ugadaga.
	Naval base started Sept. 1940 by civilian contractor; transferred to naval construction troops in July 1942; cost about $44 million. Fort Mears, Jan. 1941-June 1944, by contractor Siems Drake Puget Sound and Seabees. Army facilities on Amaknak Island turned over to Navy in Aug. 1942, and Army relocated to Unalaska Island; cost $12.3 million.	Various naval units and visiting ships; Patrol Wing Four PBY squadrons including VP-41, VP-42, VP-61; Army units included 151st Combat Engineers; 264th and 206th Coast Artillery Battalions.	Navy base decommissioned in 1947; federal government started auctioning military parcels in 1960s; halted after protest from residents; most eventually transferred to Native village corporation; designated NHL, Feb. 1985.

■ **FORT GLENN / CAPE FIELD / NAVAL AIR FACILITY** (Cape Field at Fort Glenn NHL) Umnak Island Army airfield at Otter Point, east end of Umnak, built in secret to protect Dutch Harbor naval base, 70 miles east; also naval air facility; housing for about 10,580 men; hospital; fuel, bomb and ammunition storage; 3 main runways with an additional 6 at satellite fields; steel Marston matting used here first as runway surface. Airfield named after fighter pilot Lt. John Cape Jr., shot down by enemy in June 4, 1942 dogfight.	Spring 1941-early 1944, by Army engineers and Sea-bees; shipments addressed to fictitious fish cannery to thwart enemy; supplies landed at Chernofski Harbor, 12 miles away, and barged to airfield; abnormally high 45 percent lumber breakage from repeated handling; cost about $18 million.	Army units of 802nd and 807th Engineer Aviation Battalions, 93rd Combat Engineers, 138th Infantry, anti-aircraft and field artillery; units of Eleventh Air Force including 11th Fighter Squadron, 36th and 77th Bomber Squadrons; Patrol Wing Four PBYs including VP-41.	Vacated by military in late 1940s; some land transferred to state in 1966 under act allowing states to reclaim airfields; used for sheep ranching in 1950s and 1960s; some parcels transferred to Native corporations; designated NHL, May 1987.
■ **FORT RANDALL / THORNBOROUGH ARMY AIRFIELD / NAVAL SECTION BASE** Cold Bay Forward air base with coastal defenses; built in secret to defend Aleutians and mainland; also Navy base to service vessels and seaplanes; staging field for Attu invasion and air attacks on Kiska; Lend-Lease ships transferred here in 1945; Russian naval crews trained in Operation HULA. Airfield named for pilot Capt. George W. Thornborough, who crashed in mission against Japanese after Dutch Harbor attack.	Aug. 1941-Dec. 1943, by Morrison-Knudsen under CAA, transferred to Army engineers in Feb. 1942; equipment and supplies addressed to fictitious cannery; cost about $20 million.	Units of 151st and 93rd Engineers; 53rd and 138th Infantry; 75th, 161st and 209th Field Artillery; 203rd and 30th Coast Artillery; 260th Port Battalion; Eleventh Air Force fighters and bombers; Patrol Wing Four PBYs including VP-42; various naval units and visiting ships.	Fort Randall abandoned; airfield operated by Army; transferred to Reeve Aleutian Airlines; used as military supply base during Korean War; operated by Flying Tigers in 1960s; Air Force refueling stop during Vietnam War; town of Cold Bay has about 150 people, most employed by federal government; important regional air hub.
■ **FORT RAYMOND / NAVAL SECTION BASE** Seward Army coastal defense for Seward and railroad terminal; housing for 3,500 men, dock, fuel loading, storage, freight handling, ship haulout and repair; Navy section base served seaplanes and boats; Army fixed harbor defense garrisons around Resurrection Bay at Caines Head (Fort McGilvray) and Rugged Island; searchlight, fire control and housing at Rocky Point, Topeka Point, Carol Cove, Chamberlain Point, Barwell Island and Alama Point; seacoast radar at Patsy Point and South Beach; naval facility transferred to U.S. Coast Guard in July 1943.	July 1941-Nov. 1943 (Feb. 1944 for coastal defenses), by Army engineers and West Construction Co.; building coastal defenses complicated by steep granite coastline; i.e., tramway built to hoist materials up the slopes of Mary Bay; total cost exceeded $11 million; dismantled in mid-1944.	Units of 151st Combat Engineers; 250th Coast Artillery; 267th Separate Coast Artillery Regiment; 220th Anti-Aircraft Battery; 153rd Infantry; various naval units.	Seward residents scavenged building materials from abandoned installations; state selected land at Caines Head in 1971; today Caines Head State Recreation Area has nearly 6,000 acres.

NAME / LOCATION / DESCRIPTION:	CONSTRUCTION:*	SERVED HERE:	AFTER THE WAR:

■ **FORT RICHARDSON / ELMENDORF FIELD**
Anchorage
 	
    Fort Richardson: Army headquarters for Alaska Defense Command; central air base, ground garrison and supply base for southern Alaska. Named for Brig. Gen. Wilds P. Richardson, former head of Alaska Road Commission.
    Elmendorf Field: Initial headquarters of Eleventh Air Force located on Fort Richardson; planes patrolled lower Cook Inlet to Yakutat and rotated to forward bases; first commanding officer, Maj. (later Col.) Everett S. Davis, Feb. 1942; succeeded by Gen. William O. Butler. Named for pilot Capt. Hugh M. Elmendorf, killed in 1933 air crash at Wright Field, Ohio.
	June 1940-1944, by contractor Bechtel-McCone-Parson and Army engineers; included railroad spur; cost $45 million.	Units of 28th Composite Group; 4th Infantry Regiment; combat support including 65th Coast Artillery; Eleventh Air Force including 23rd Air Base Group, 36th, 73rd and 77th Bomber Squadrons, 18th Pursuit Squadron, 42nd and 54th Troop Carrier Squadrons; Royal Canadian Air Force squadrons.	Transferred to Air Force in 1950s; new Fort Richardson constructed nearby. Today, Fort Richardson is headquarters for U.S. Army in Alaska; major units include 1st Battalion (Airborne 501st Infantry Regiment) and Arctic Support Brigade. Today, Elmendorf is the largest Air Force installation in Alaska and headquarters of the Eleventh Air Force; host unit is the 3rd Wing.

■ **KISKA NAVAL FACILITY / ARMY AIRFIELD**
   (Japanese Occupation Site, Kiska Island NHL)
Kiska Island
 	
    Forward base built after Americans reclaimed island; one runway, ship and barge docks, 225-bed hospital; naval air facility included seaplane ramps and support services.
	Aug. 1943-June 1944, by Army engineers; originally planned for 15,000 men, but downsized to about 400; cost $3 million.	<u>Invasion forces:</u> Alaska Scouts; units of 7th Infantry Division; 87th Mountain Combat Team; 13th RCAF Infantry Brigade; 785th Battery and 24th Field Regiment of RCAF Artillery; 1st Special Service Force (American and Canadian paratroopers and amphibious troops); 196th Signal Photo Co.; 762nd Aircraft Warning Co; various Navy units and Eleventh Air Force squadrons. <u>Post-invasion:</u> 38th Naval Construction Battalion; units of Eleventh Air Force and Navy.	Abandoned by military; designated NHL, Feb. 1985; memorial plaque erected in 1987 by Mountain Infantry veterans; National Park Service documented war relics in Kiska Harbor, 1989.

■ **KODIAK NAVAL OPERATING BASE / FORT GREELY**
   (Kodiak Naval Operating Base and
   Forts Greely and Abercrombie NHL)
Kodiak Island
 	
    Principal advance naval base at start of war; joint operations center directed Alaska operations early 1942-March 1943; its ships and submarines played critical role in Aleutian campaign; included naval air station, runways, seaplane ramps, submarine base, net depot, ammunition and fuel storage, docks, piers, warehouses, Marine barracks, recreational facilities; first commander of Alaska Naval Sector at Kodiak, Capt. Ralph C. Parker.
    Fort Greely garrisoned for coastal defense of naval base; troops arrived April 1941; top strength more than 11,000 men; Army planes used runways on naval base; fixed defense garrisons included Fort Abercrombie at Miller Point, Fort Tidball on Long Island, and Fort J.H. Smith at Cape Chiniak; searchlights, fire control, radar installations, gun emplacements and magazines at numerous points and capes throughout Kodiak archipelago. Named for Arctic explorer Maj. Gen. Adolphus W. Greely.
	Sept. 1939-June 1944 by Siems Drake Puget Sound and Seabees (who took over in 1943); naval base cost about $70 million; Fort Greely cost exceeded $17.6 million.	Patrol Wing Four units including VP-41, VP-42, VP-43, VB-45, VP-51, VB-135, VB-136; various naval units and visiting ships; units of Eleventh Air Force; Royal Canadian Air Force bombers and fighters starting Oct. 1942; 151st Combat Engineers, 69th Quartermaster Battalion; 37th and 201st Infantry; 9th and 10th Ordnance Service Regiments; 65th, 215th, 250th and 265th Coast Artillery; 98th and 30th Field Artillery; 862nd Anti-Aircraft Artillery; 374th Port Battalion; 114th Signal Service Co.	Submarine base decommissioned May 1945; naval air station remained active during Cold War; transferred to U.S. Coast Guard in 1971; today largest Coast Guard station in nation, with search and rescue patrols for Bering Sea and North Pacific; Panama gun mounts still visible on Buskin Hill, leased by the state for Buskin State Recreation Site; gun mounts and relics visible at Fort Abercrombie State Historical Park; designated NHL, Feb. 1985.

NAME / LOCATION / DESCRIPTION:	CONSTRUCTION:*	SERVED HERE:	AFTER THE WAR:
■ **LADD FIELD** (Ladd Field [Fort Wainwright] NHL) Fairbanks Alaska's first Army airfield, built for cold-weather testing; became Air Transport Command headquarters and main staging base for Lend-Lease aircraft transfers to Soviet Union. Named for pilot Maj. Arthur K. Ladd, killed in 1935 air crash in South Carolina.	Summer 1939-Oct. 1944, by Army engineers; airfield operational Sept. 1940; included railroad spur from Fairbanks; Mile 26 Satellite Field, built southeast of Fairbanks by Morrison-Knudsen Co. in 1943 to handle Lend-Lease overflow; $25 million total cost.	Units of 151st Combat Engineers; 123rd Army Airways Communication System Squadron; units of Air Transport Command.	Mile 26 Satellite field was expanded and renamed Eielson Air Force Base in 1948; today Eielson hosts 354th Fighter Wing of Eleventh Air Force. Ladd Field transferred to Army in 1961; renamed Fort Wainwright after Gen. Jonathan Wainwright captured in Philippines in WWII; designated NHL, Feb. 1985. Today home of 1st Brigade 6th Infantry Division Light.
■ **SHEMYA ARMY AIRFIELD / NAVAL AIR FACILITY** Shemya Island Built during Attu battle as intermediate Army and Navy air base between Attu and Amchitka islands; advance Army base for attacks on Kuriles; housing for about 10,000 men with 450-bed hospital; 2 paved runways, fuel storage, hangars, warehousing.	June 1943-Nov. 1944; cost about $15 million.	Units of 18th Engineers; Eleventh Air Force squadrons including 28th and 77th Bomber Squadrons and 11th, 18th, 53rd, 344th Fighter Squadrons; Patrol Wing Four PBYs.	Continued operating until 1951; leased to Northwest Orient Airlines for refueling stop; used for military refueling during Korean War; important Air Force base during Cold War for strategic intelligence gathering; Cobra Dane radar facility built in 1970s to monitor missile activities and earth satellites; named Eareckson Air Force Station in 1993, after Col. William O. Eareckson, head of Army Air bomber command during WWII; closed in 1995 with runways maintained for emergency use.
■ **SITKA NAVAL OPERATING BASE / FORT RAY / FORT ROUSSEAU** (Sitka Naval Operating Base and U.S. Army Coastal Defenses NHL) Japonski Island, Sitka Alaska's first Navy air station and one of few prepared to protect North Pacific during first months of war; its seaplanes patrolled Southeast and Gulf of Alaska for enemy activity; intermediate stop for planes flying along the coast; redesignated as operating base in July 1942; made air station in March 1943; modern, well-equipped base with comfortable living accommodations and "magnificent" views from every window, according to a Seabee in 1943. Fort Ray on Charcoal and Alice islands anchored harbor defense of naval base; named for Brig. Gen. Patrick H. Ray, stationed at Sitka as lieutenant in 1897 to register food supplies of gold prospectors. Fort Rousseau on Makhnati Island coastal defense headquarters; linked to Japonski by 8,100-foot rock-fill causeway across seven intermediate islands; leveled for buildings, warehouses and barracks. Other coastal defense included Fort Babcock, at Shoals Point on Kruzof Island; Fort Pierce on Biorka Island; and gun batteries at Olga and Watson points and Whale Island; radar, searchlights and fire-control stations located on numerous other islands.	Navy seaplane base built in 1937 on Navy property (patrol ship base 1879 to 1884, with coaling station built in 1902); expanded in 1939, by contractors and Seabees (in Nov. 1942); cost about $32 million; decommissioned Aug. 15, 1944. Army posts built Jan. 1941-July 1944, by contractor Siems Drake Puget Sound and Army engineers; cost exceeded $9.9 million. Causeway July 1941-Feb. 1943; cost $2 million; constant repairs of damage from currents, waves and storms.	Various naval ships; Patrol Wing Four squadrons including VP-41, VP-42; 22nd Naval Construction Battalion; Army units from Chilkoot Barracks in May 1941; 151st Combat Engineers.	Naval reservation transferred in 1947 to Bureau of Indian Affairs for Mount Edgecumbe boarding school; now state-operated school, still uses some WWII buildings; U.S. Public Health Service hospital on old naval base site; U.S. Coast Guard Air Station on northwest end of Japonski; Sitka city airport across head of state-owned causeway; designated NHL, Aug. 1986.

Other Military Installations

AKUTAN ISLAND NAVY REFUELING DEPOT
Established Feb. 1943 at former Akutan whaling station; supplied coal and oil to Soviet ships transporting Lend-Lease supplies to Russia; included housing, docks, coal handling facilities, signal lights; adjunct to Dutch Harbor naval base.

ANNETTE ISLAND ARMY AIRFIELD/ NAVAL AIR FACILITY
Intermediate landing field and staging base between Lower 48 and Alaska for bomber and fighter planes; included runways, seaplane ramps, hangars, coastal defense gun batteries, housing for Royal Canadian Air Force 115th Fighter Squadron, Army and Navy units. Constructed July 1940-May 1943, by Army engineers with permission from reservation land-owner Metlakatla Village; included road to village; cost $8.8 million.

CHILKOOT BARRACKS, Haines
Built in 1903 during gold rush as Fort William Henry Seward; renamed Chilkoot Barracks in 1920s; enlarged April 1942-May 1943 at a cost of $115,000, for troop training and as rest and recreation center; housing for

570 men; 30-bed hospital; wartime units included 4th and 297th Infantry; after the war in 1947, the fort was purchased by five WWII veterans, renamed Port Chilkoot, and developed as a planned community; annexed by City of Haines in 1970; added to the National Register of Historic Sites in 1972 as Fort William H. Seward, because of its gold rush significance; designated NHL, June 1978.

CORDOVA NAVAL SECTION BASE
Established July 1942 for repair of small craft; ordnance storage magazines built under Army supervision; later transferred to the U.S. Coast Guard.

FALSE PASS NAVAL SECTION BASE
Established July 1941 but never activated; construction and operating funds transferred to Cold Bay in July 1942.

FORT MORROW, Port Heiden
Army airfield for defense of Dutch Harbor; housing for 455 men; 2 runways, barge dock, fuel storage, warehouses, hangars, hospital; constructed July 1942-Dec. 1943; cost $5.58 million.

KETCHIKAN NAVAL SECTION BASE
Established July 1941 under direction of U.S. Coast Guard; transferred to Coast Guard in Oct. 1942.

PORT ARMSTRONG NAVAL SECTION BASE Baranof Island
Established July 1941 at former herring reduction plant to service seaplanes and small boats; designated Naval Air Facility in 1943; closed Aug. 1943.

PORT ALTHORP NAVAL SECTION BASE, Chichagof Island
Established July 1941; included seaplane ramp, minor repair facility, storage, housing, recreational facilities; designated Auxiliary Air Facility in March 1943.

SAND BAY NAVAL FUELING STATION, Great Sitkin Island
Built May 1943 by Seabees as advance fueling station; adjunct to Adak naval base.

SAND POINT NAVAL SECTION BASE, Popof Island
Established at former cannery for seaplane tenders; designated Naval Auxiliary Air Facility in Feb. 1943; closed Aug. 1943.

ST. PAUL ISLAND ARMY AIRFIELD
Airfield built to defend Bristol Bay and mainland from Bering Sea; housed 1,400 men in tents and village homes vacated by government's evacuation of Aleuts; constructed Sept. 1942-June 1943, when project abandoned; runway and radio station destroyed by explosions and Army buildings torn down for reuse elsewhere; cost about $300,000.

TANAGA ISLAND LANDING STRIP
Built July 1943 by Seabees as emergency landing strip.

VALDEZ ARMY GARRISON
Port operating garrison; handled freight for construction in Interior; also defense of Port of Valdez; housing for 260 men; constructed April 1943-Oct. 1943; cost $392,000.

YAKUTAT ARMY AIRFIELD/ NAVAL SECTION BASE
Built as intermediate field between Alaska and Lower 48 for bomber and fighter planes; launched Gulf of Alaska patrols; constructed Sept. 1940-June 1943 by Army engineers; used Libby, McNeil & Libby cannery 10-mile railroad to haul supplies; cost $10 million; naval base established July 1941; downgraded to naval auxiliary air facility in Feb. 1943.

Civilian Aeronautics Administration/ Army Air Transport Command Airfields
   (Airfields built by civilian contractors; garrisons built by Army engineers)

MARKS AIR FORCE BASE, Nome
Operating base for bomber and fighter patrols of Bering Sea and Alaska's west coast; Alaska National Guard and Royal Canadian Air Force squadron stationed here; 3 CAA runways expanded for Lend-Lease aircraft. Named for Maj. Jack Marks, a B-17 pilot shot down over Kiska; constructed July 1941-Aug. 1944 by units of 32nd Engineers; built 2 miles northwest of town; Army operated 10 miles of Seward Peninsula narrow-gauge railroad during construction; cost about $7 million.

CORDOVA AIRFIELD
Airfield located 13 miles southeast of town on former railroad frontage; included 1 runway and housing for 1,080 men; built March 1942-June 1943 by units of 42nd Engineers; Army operated 13 miles of abandoned Copper River & Northwestern Railroad during construction; cost about $1.86 million.

■ **JUNEAU AIRFIELD**
Located 6 miles from town; housing for 1,100 men; 1 runway; constructed March 1942-June 1943 by units of 42nd Engineers; cost $1.1 million.

■ **NAKNEK AIRFIELD**
Built 15 miles up Naknek River from Bristol Bay; housing for 1,370 men; constructed July 1942-Sept. 1943 by units of 176th Engineers; supplies lightered from ships anchored 14 miles offshore, then towed upriver during high tides; cost about $1.5 million; site today holds King Salmon airport.

■ **GULKANA AIRFIELD**
Located 9 miles south on Richardson Hwy.; housing for 490 men, 14-bed hospital, Alaska Communications System facilities; constructed July 1942-July 1943 by units of 176th Engineers; cost about $453,000.

■ **BETHEL AIRFIELD**
Infantry and Air Corps garrisons located near Bethel; housing for 750 men; 2 runways; constructed by units of 176th Engineers, July 1942-Sept. 1943 when halted incomplete; cost $1.5 million.

■ **BIG DELTA AIRFIELD**
Located 90 miles east of Ladd Field on Tanana River, near Richardson Hwy.; constructed July 1942-1943 by units of 176th Engineers; cost about $1.74 million housing for 900 men; 14-bed hospital; expanded by Air Transport Command as ferry route for Lend-Lease aircraft; reactivated in 1948; now U.S. Cold Region Test Center at Fort Greely.

■ **NORTHWAY AIRFIELD**
Part of Lend-Lease transfer route; housing for about 150 men with 4-bed hospital; 1 CAA runway extended and paved; constructed July 1942-June 1943 by units of 176th Engineers; cost about $585,000.

■ **McGRATH AIRFIELD**
Intermediate airfield between Anchorage and Nome, and Fairbanks and Bethel; located on Kuskokwim River; housing for about 180 men; small hospital; 2 paved runways; constructed July 1942-July 1943 by units of 176th Engineers; cost about $710,000.

■ **MOSES POINT AIRFIELD**
Single runway emergency landing field; at mouth of Kwiniuk River on Norton Sound; originally planned for 1,200 men with 50-bed hospital; downgraded to 150 men and 6-bed hospital; constructed Sept.-Nov. 1942 by units of 297th Infantry; cost about $367,000.

■ **GALENA AIRFIELD**
Intermediate landing field between Fairbanks and Nome; part of the Air Transport Command ferry route for Lend-Lease aircraft; housing for 350 men; 12-bed hospital; 2 runways; constructed Sept. 1942-Aug. 1944 by units of 176th Engineers; second runway contracted to Summers Construction Co. of Juneau; cost about $714,000.

■ **TANACROSS AIRFIELD**
Part of Air Transport Command's ferry route for Lend-Lease aircraft; located 150 miles east of Fairbanks, 2 miles off Alaska Hwy.; housing for 50 men; 2 gravel runways; Constructed Nov. 1942-June 1943 by units of 176th Engineers; cost about $130,000.

Other Military Projects

■ **WHITTIER / Railroad Spur, Tunnel and Dock**
Army port in Whittier on Prince William Sound built primarily as backup to Seward port; railroad spur connected Whittier with Alaska Railroad at Portage; included dock, warehouses, cold storage, rail repair, housing for 1,150 men, 50-bed hospital, recreational facilities.

First of 3 construction phases started June 1941 by West Construction Co.; railroad completed April 1943; cost more than $16 million.

Assigned troops: units of 42nd, 151st and 177th Engineers; 714th Railroad Battalion; 778th Track Maintenance Platoon.

Facilities transferred to Alaska Railroad in 1945, returned to Army in 1946; Army built large concrete high-rise for family housing and a multipurpose building to house troops and essential services in the 1950s; operated port facilities until 1960; Whittier now town of about 280 people with overland rail link to road system.

■ **ALASKA HIGHWAY**
Built by military in 1942 to join Alaska to Lower 48 by road; connected Army Air Transport Command airfields; 1,200 miles through Canada and 200 miles into Alaska; pioneer road completed in just over 8 months; Army continued improvements until 1943 when work transferred to 70 civilian contracting companies; 160-mile connecting road from Haines built in 1943; Skagway and Valdez were entry ports for troops and supplies; main construction camp in Whitehorse; Alcan cost exceeded $135 million; Haines Cutoff exceeded $13 million.

Troops assigned: Units of 35th, 87th, 18th and the all-black 93rd, 95th and 97th Engineer regiments; 340th and 341st General Service Regiments; 73rd Light Pontoon Company; 29th Topographic Battalion; the 770th Railway Operating Battalion (manned White Pass and Yukon Route railroad out of Skagway from Oct. 1942-Oct. 1944).

Canadian authorities took control of their segment April 1946; road opened year-round with tourist facilities in 1949.

■ **CANOL**
Built by Army with consent of Canada; included roads and pipelines from MacKenzie River oil fields in Northwest Territories (operated by Imperial Oil Co. of Canada) to refinery in Whitehorse (operated by Standard Oil Co. of Ca.); included Canol 2 fuel pipeline from Skagway to Whitehorse, Canol 3 fuel pipeline to Watson Lake, and Canol 4 fuel pipeline to Tanacross and Fairbanks; also 3,000-mile telephone line connecting Fairbanks, Norman Wells and Helena, Mt.; Skagway port expanded with Army garrison to handle incoming shipments.

Construction on main line started June 1942 by civilian contracting consortium (W.A. Bechtel Co. of San Francisco, H.C. Price Co. of Bartlesville, Okla., and W.E. Callahan Co. of Dallas); Canol 2, 3 and 4 fuel pipelines completed in 1943; main Canol pipeline completed in April 1944; costs exceeded $135 million.

Troops assigned: Units of 388th and 35th Engineers; 90th Heavy Pontoon Battalion.

Canol shut down June 1945; pipeline sold in 1947 for $700,000 to private companies and dismantled; Imperial Oil bought refinery for $1 million, relocated it to Alberta.

■ **JUNEAU / Excursion Inlet Port**
Deep water port on Icy Strait, northwest of Juneau; used as barge terminal to transfer goods out of Seattle and British Columbia onto ships for Kodiak and Aleutians; expanded as major support base for operations in Aleutians; housing for 3,730 men, 200-bed hospital; 3 docks units each with fuel storage, sheds, warehouses.

Constructed Aug. 1942-March 1943 by contractor Guy F. Atkinson Co. of San Francisco and units of 331st Engineers; cost about $36.8 million; closed down April 1944; dismantled in 1945 by German prisoners-of-war from camp in Colorado.

Fifty Year Memories

By Rob Carson

FACING PAGE:
The five senior officers at Dutch Harbor the day it was bombed pose for a photo. At center stands Carl Eric "Squeaky" Anderson, a barrel-shaped, barely-more-than-5-feet-tall seaman with a voice described as similar to the sound of a tired fog-horn. Squeaky was beachmaster in charge of landing supplies and equipment for the Attu and Kiska assaults, and then was assigned to the invasions in the Central Pacific including Iwo Jima and Okinawa. He retired from the Navy as a rear admiral. (Courtesy of Reeve Aleutian Airways)

Editor's note: *In 1941, VP42, a Navy squadron of Catalina flying boats, had been sent north to Alaska from Seattle. With the seaplane tender USS Williamson, they flew throughout the Aleutian chain and became the first planes to operate out of the new naval air station at Dutch Harbor. VP42 eventually settled in Kodiak, where they remained until October, when they returned to Seattle for training and equipment. By January 1942 VP42 was headed back to Alaska, this time flying PBY5-As, the amphibious version of the Catalina. From late January to late May 1942, VP42 was "the only reconnaissance squadron covering the Alaskan seas," according to its commander, retired Adm. James S. Russell. VP42 and VP41 were at Dutch Harbor on June 3, 1942, when Japanese bombs brought World War II to Alaska.*

On Labor Day Weekend 1995, the Eleventh Air Force Association and the Navy Patwing 4 Association held a joint 50th reunion for veterans of the Aleutian Campaign in Tacoma, Wash. Rob Carson, military-affairs reporter for The News Tribune *in Tacoma attended the reunion and interviewed some of the veterans.*

We thank the many veterans who shared their memories and their photos of those days a half-century ago, especially Jack Haugen, an enlisted flight captain with Squadron VP43 operating from Attu and Shemya islands in 1943 and 1944.

Hiroichi Samejima

Hiroichi Samejima's job on June 3, 1942, was to destroy the American fighter base at Dutch Harbor.

He was 24 at the time, commander of a squadron of bombers in a Japanese carrier group that had steamed undetected into the Aleutians.

There were two major difficulties with the mission, Samejima discovered. One was the weather. "Visibility was very bad. The ceiling was maybe 300 feet."

The other problem was worse: There was no fighter base at Dutch Harbor.

"This was a big problem in our intelligence,"

Samejima said. "Our submarines said this is where it is."

In fact, the American fighters were based on Umnak Island, more than 50 miles southwest.

"I was commander of the first attack unit, consisting of seven 'Kate' bombers and three Zero 'Whites,'" Samejima remembered.

With Samejima in the lead, they took off in the dark and flew the 180 miles to Dutch Harbor just above the water, to avoid the clouds. At Dutch Harbor, the clouds cleared and they soared into clear blue sky.

"We could see everything clearly," Samejima said. "I could see Dutch Harbor Bay. But not an airfield.

Commodore Leslie E. Gehres, USN, commanding officer of Fleet Air Wing Four, prepares to board a PBY5-A at Adak, December 1943. (Courtesy of Jack Haugen)

I could not find it. I asked my crew, but they also did not see the airfield."

Disappointed, Samejima sent his planes after less satisfying targets — a radio shack, a barracks, a few Navy pontoon boats moored in the bay.

On their way back to their ships, some of the Japanese fighters were attacked by American P-40s. Samejima said his commander was furious.

He sent Samejima back on a reconnaissance mission.

"I searched until fuel ran low. But again, I had to report, 'I am sorry, I cannot find the airfield.'"

The following day, a Japanese Zero pilot accidentally discovered the hidden airfield on Umnak Island while pursuing American P-40s.

But by then it was too late, Samejima said.

"I wanted to bomb it, but our commanding officer said we were returning to sea. I couldn't understand why."

Later, Samejima learned that his commander had received an urgent order to help out at the battle of Midway, where Japanese naval forces were being pounded by Americans.

As it turned out, they were too late there as well.

Wylie Hunt

When bullets from the Japanese Zeroes hit Wylie Hunt's patrol plane, he said it sounded like a sudden burst of hail.

Hunt never saw the enemy planes. But he knew immediately what had happened.

"They shot out an engine right away. Maybe both engines. The next thing I knew, we were on our way down."

As his PBY plummeted to the waves below, Hunt rolled up into a ball on the floor. "Then we hit the water."

Hunt, the co-pilot and navigator of the PBY, had

been in the Aleutians less than a week at that time. He was on his first reconnaissance flight out of the secret U.S. airstrip on Umnak Island, and he was unlucky enough to have flown into the Japanese combat air patrol surrounding the carrier *Junyo*.

"When we stopped, I jumped up and started back to the waist hatch where we could get out," Hunt remembers.

"On the way back, I passed by where the small, two-man raft was kept and so I picked it up and took it with me. I got out of the airplane and got out on the wing and launched the raft and got in it."

With the plane quickly filling with water, the rest of the crew worked frantically with a larger, eight-man raft, trying to get it launched. "It was all shot full of holes and wouldn't hold any air at all. So they couldn't get it to float."

Three men sank out of sight with the large raft. The remaining three splashed through the icy water to Hunt.

"We got a couple of them aboard. A couple of them hung onto the side, but it was so cold they didn't last very long. The pilot had been wounded so he died very quickly. That left three of us in the raft."

Soaking wet and freezing, the three men drifted on the raft, so small it was barely able to keep them afloat. After six or seven hours, Hunt said, the Japanese cruiser *Takao* appeared through the fog and spotted them.

"They sailed the ship right up beside us. They tossed a rope down to us and hung a ladder over the side."

Hunt and one of the other men were able to climb the ladder without help. The third man was so exhausted he had to be hauled up by a rope tied around his chest.

On deck, Japanese crewmen surrounded the three Americans and hustled them to a secure compartment below.

FAW4- 56809-43   LOOKING   005°.   N.W. PT. OF   CAPE WRANGELL , ATTU.
F-56   of 1 8½'   ALT. 3,500'   9-5-43

Cape Wrangell, Attu, is the westernmost tip of the Aleutians. Next stop for Allied pilots or sailors venturing beyond was either the Japanese-held Kuriles Islands or the Soviet Union's Siberia. (U.S. Government photo, courtesy of Jack Haugen)

The Japanese planes that had attacked Dutch Harbor that morning were unable to find an airfield, yet they had been attacked by American fighter planes.

Hunt's captors demanded that he tell them where the American fighters had come from. Hunt feigned ignorance, even though he knew full well the American fighters were using the hastily constructed strip on Umnak, where he himself had departed that morning.

Hunt told them his plane had taken off from the water at Dutch Harbor and insisted he didn't know anything about any other airfield.

"They had men with bayonets standing over me and they were asking questions and so on. I told them I had been in Dutch Harbor such a short period of time I didn't know anything about the place. And I didn't."

Enraged, the Japanese threatened to kill Hunt if he didn't talk.

"They took me up on the deck and tied a weight around my waist and put me out on a little platform over the ocean. They said, 'We'll shove you in if you don't tell us what we want to know.' It was sort of like walking the plank.

"I thought I was a goner anyway, so I thought, 'I'm not going to tell them anything because they're going to kill me anyway.' I told them I didn't know, and if they were going to shove me in then let me talk to a priest or minister first."

Hunt convinced them.

"They pulled me back in from the platform, out of the ocean, and took me down below again."

Hunt maintained his ignorance about the secret airstrip for a week and a half as the *Takao* sailed back to Japan, and later at an interrogation camp, even though he was beaten.

One day his captors told him they had found out all about the base at Umnak. Soon after, Hunt was transferred to a regular prison camp, where he spent the rest of the war.

"I think that's the main reason they picked us up out of the ocean," Hunt said. "They wanted information about the area up there."

Luke Watkins

By the time Luke Watkins got to Attu, the island had been retaken by Americans. Not all the Japanese soldiers had been rounded up yet though, and Watkins remembers they would occasionally wander out of the hills and into the base, hungry and cold.

"They would get into Army fatigues, and they'd even get in the chow lines. The cooks would get them sometimes. They'd hear them rattling around in the garbage pails."

Japanese fighters were still airborne as well, as Watkins and the rest of his crew quickly found out.

Watkins was an aviation ordinance man in Squadron VP43, and he had a reputation as one of the best gunners in the outfit.

He got a chance to prove it in what turned out to be the last Japanese combat action in the Aleutians. It was a duel between a fast and deadly Japanese "Betty" and Watkins' ungainly PBY, a mismatch that lives in legend among Aleutian veterans.

"We had been on a patrol, and we were on the way to the base. We [weren't] too far out. I'm not sure how far we were, but we were on our way back to the base and here come a Betty.

"I don't know if you know anything about the Betty. It was supposed to be one of the best twin-engine light bombers, very heavily armed. Of course it spotted us.

"The first I knew, it came over the intercom from the co-pilot. He just said, 'Man your battle stations.' That's the only words he said. He didn't say what it was.

"My first reaction was that it was a submarine, so I armed all the bombs. Then one of our 50s [50mm guns] in the back opened up. When I heard the gun roaring from the back, I knew it was a plane.

"My battle station was in the blister up front. I scooted headfirst between the pilots and got on the turret guns.

"Now, of course, the Japanese, they're smart people. They had studied the PBY, I'm sure, because they come at you where you can't train your guns at them. In the bow position you have to be careful that you don't shoot your own props off, because you certainly can.

"They come in very close. On the second run, they made a run head on and then they circled back and come up on the port side. They were staying in behind the plane enough to where it was difficult to get a real good shot."

Navy hangars and PBY5-As of Navy squadron VP62 await duty on Amchitka Island. (U.S. Government photo, courtesy of Jack Haugen)

Thanks to the skill of Watkins' pilot, Glenn Violette, the PBY avoided the deadly tail of the Betty. "They have a 20mm cannon in the tail. That's what they want to try to get you with. But our pilot, he knew that, and he evaded it.

Incredibly, Watkins managed to squeeze in some accurate split-second shots.

"They pulled away, came back at us from the port, into the bow, circled back and came in from the starboard."

Again Watkins fired. "Then they broke off the attack."

"I'm satisfied we got some good shots in. They wouldn't have broken it off like they did if they hadn't been riddled pretty good."

Watkins' plane took some heavy hits, too.

"They shot the plexiglass out right above the co-pilot's head. And there was one bullet that went right between the legs of the head mechanic.

"Our navigator passed the camera up to the co-pilot. He was going to take a picture of it. Unfortunately, there wasn't any film in the camera, we found out.

"He wanted to get a picture to prove it happened. Course you didn't need to prove it, all you had to do was just look at the bullet holes." ■

ATG: Alaska's Patriotic Militia

By Chris Wooley and Mike Martz

FACING PAGE:
The exploits of Maj. "Muktuk" Marston and the Alaska Territorial Guard caught the attention of military artists covering war activities in Alaska. This painting, Major Marston Arms the Eskimos, by Henry Varnum Poor depicts the major issuing weapons to members of the ATG. Poor was a member of the Army Art Unit, one of several American and Canadian artists sent to Alaska to record military activities. (Courtesy of The Center of Military History)

Editor's note: *Chris Wooley is a consulting anthropologist who has worked in coastal British Columbia and throughout Alaska for the past 15 years. Mike Martz is the executive producer for public television station KYUK in Bethel. He has been with the station since 1982.*

When Japan attacked Pearl Harbor in 1941, shock waves rumbled across the country. The possibility of a Japanese invasion was especially disturbing in the Territory of Alaska, particularly in villages of the Yukon-Kuskokwim delta, Northwest Alaska and on the North Slope. Although the region wasn't a military target, it was a huge and remote area close to Asia that had no defense force on the ground. It also happened to be the homeland of Yup'ik and Inupiat people. The villagers' vigorous response reflects the rich communal life in Native communities in the late 1930s and early 1940s. Elderly former militia volunteers recollect those days — with purposeful gestures and an occasional self-deprecating anecdote — when they describe volunteering as "Uncle Sam's Men" for the Alaska Territorial Guard.

The Alaska Territorial Guard, or ATG (known locally as the "Tundra Army"), was formed in the spring of 1942 following the Japanese bombing of Dutch Harbor and the capture of Attu and Kiska islands. The original Alaska National Guard, the 297th Infantry Battalion, was in federal service at the time and the 77th Congress authorized the formation of a territorial militia to assist in the defense of Alaska. Maj. Marvin "Muktuk" Marston, an Army Air Corps officer assigned to Fort Richardson in Anchorage, was designated one of two military liaison officers for Territorial Gov. Ernest Gruening. Marston's task was the military organization of the predominately Eskimo villages west of the 154th parallel along the Bering Sea and Arctic coasts. During the next three years, using surplus World War I weapons and equipment, Marston helped establish a defense force, from Barrow to Bristol Bay, comprised

Pilots worked in shifts so the planes could fly around the clock during the long, darkless, summer days. This was the largest airlift of its time; 1,100 tons of supplies and 300 construction workers were flown into the Northway site in less than five months. The supplies included 2,800 barrels of asphalt for the paving of the completed runway. In the spring of 1942, the Army began to greatly expand the facilities and construction continued at a frantic pace. New facilities included a theater, church, aircraft hangar, barracks and many more buildings. The Army gave contracts to several local traders for the lumber needed for the added buildings and soon sawmills were operating in several nearby areas in an all-out effort to supply the Army with as much lumber as necessary. The larger timbers and specialty items had to be hauled in by aircraft, boat, or by road after the winter of 1942 when the

TOP:
Cooks, kitchen help and waitresses gather at Northway in 1944. (Courtesy of Lavell Wilson)

LEFT:
This photo shows beginning construction of the first permanent building at the Tanacross airport. The Stout prefab houses and other buildings were used for worker housing. The truck parked at extreme left indicates that at least a winter road to Tanacross was open at this time, which Lavell Wilson estimates to be 1942. (Courtesy of Lavell Wilson)

first truck convoys made it through on the Alcan.

Following the Pearl Harbor attack, which occurred several months after the Northway airport was begun, the military realized how important these facilities were in the overall defense of Alaska and the rest of the country. They

learned also that the Northway site did have some problems. Northway had no highway link as yet for supplies brought to Alaska by ship or truck. Officials were not sure when, or if, the Alcan would be usable. Soil conditions were poor for any expansion of the existing runway. Construction of any cross-wind or additional runways was not feasible. So, within a few weeks of the Pearl Harbor disaster, a plan was in place to construct another airport near Northway that could be reached overland in the event the Alcan project was not completed or usable.

This airport would be located about 60 miles northwest of Northway near the village of Tanacross. Situated at the Tanana River crossing of the old Valdez-Eagle Trail, Tanacross had a small existing airport with plenty of dry, flat ground for expansion. Cat crews started widening and

TOP RIGHT:
The construction camp for the Northway Airport spreads out on a slight rise overlooking the river. The sign says: "Northway M.H.K.C.B. Co. Camp 45." (Courtesy of Lavell Wilson)

RIGHT:
Airports along the Northwest Staging Route proved vital to planes and crews bringing supplies and Lend-Lease aircraft from the Lower 48 through Canada to Fairbanks and on to Siberia. This hangar under construction was part of the facility at Tanacross. Large wings on each side of the hangar were used, among other things, for offices and storage of aircraft parts and tools. In the late 1960s this building was dismantled and transported to Fairbanks, where it was rebuilt as the Big Dipper ice arena. (Courtesy of Lavell Wilson)

improving the old trail. The first Cats arrived at Tanacross in February 1942. The old trail had been for horses only, but the Cats quickly improved it enough that one-lane traffic could begin hauling supplies from Valdez to Tanacross. Construction began in earnest in summer 1942.

Building at both airports continued through the winter months as crews battled temperatures as low as minus 68. All available local men were put to work on the airports. Because there was a shortage of skilled labor, carpenters, cooks, plumbers, electricians, welders and other craftsmen were imported from all over the country. Most of the workers lived in tents for the first winter, and many for two winters, before enough permanent buildings were completed to house everyone. The men worked long hours, seven days a week, with time off to attend church services, when they were

ABOVE:
The soft, sandy-looking soil in this early view of the Northway airport required the large tires on Bob Reeve's Fairchild 71. Reeve purchased this plane from Coastal Airways in Juneau in 1939. Frank Barr flew this plane after Reeve bought his Boeing 80A in 1941. (Courtesy of Reeve Aleutian Airways)

LEFT:
This scene at the Tanacross airport shows the shop and warehouse area. The framework for some large structures, yet to be built, is visible in center back. The air raid sirens mounted on tripods were to warn of Japanese air attacks. (Courtesy of Lavell Wilson)

ABOVE:
Army personnel operate a cable ferry used at Big Delta when the bridge was out over the Tanana River. (Courtesy of Lavell Wilson)

ABOVE:
When the military moved into the Northway-Tanacross area, they required a prodigious amount of lumber for wartime construction. This photo shows the skidways at the Tok River sawmill. Behind the man at far left is the "donkey" that winched the logs out of the water and up the skidway; cables used to pull the logs can be seen at the man's feet. At least three of these men are Natives, probably from either Tanacross or Tetlin. Large piles of rotting slabs from the mill can still been seen in the area. (Courtesy of Lavell Wilson)

available. The Army authorized almost any expense as long as it sped completion of the airports. As soon as the Alcan reached the Northway area, a seven-mile spur was pushed through linking the airport to the highway. The Alcan now connected the air-ports at Northway, Tanacross and Big Delta. Large maintenance shops were built at the Northway junction for maintenance and repair of all types of military vehicles that were using the Alcan. Some housing was also constructed in the area.

While the Alcan was under construction and after the Japanese bombed Dutch Harbor in June 1942, workers began building an oil pipeline between Whitehorse and Fairbanks, known as CANOL 4. Pipeline camps and related facilities were built adjacent to both the Northway and Tanacross airports so fuel for aircraft, equipment and heating was readily available.

This was a real boon for the Northway airport, because prior to the completion of the Alcan, the airport's fuel had been delivered by air, or by boat in the summer. As soon as the runways were leveled and compacted, they were paved so that they could withstand the weight of the heavy military aircraft that would be landing on their way to Alaska bases, or to Russia under the Lend-Lease Program.

As construction was completed, the Army shipped in hundreds of military personnel to operate and maintain the airports. Aviation support staff, mechanics, tower operators, runway maintenance crews, powerhouse operators and all types of support personnel were assigned to the airports as they became large towns in the remote region. For most of the G.I.s, this was their first exposure to the extremes of Alaska's climate, summer highs of 90 degrees, winter temperatures as low as minus 72. Some loved it, some hated it; many could not wait to leave, while many others came back after the war to make their homes in Alaska and become permanent residents. ∎

Editor's note: *Harold K. Saur is the father of* ALASKA GEOGRAPHIC® *production director, Kathy Doogan.*

World War II in Alaska involved not only actual combat but numerous support activities. Among those support operations was a Navy expedition to search for oil in the Naval Petroleum Reserve 4 on the North Slope.

The 76,250 square miles of Alaska north of the Brooks Range is known as the North Slope. In 1944, about half of that territory — an area about the size of Indiana — lay within the reserve, which had been established in 1923. On Feb. 5, 1944, the Director of Naval Petroleum Reserves, Rear Adm. H.A. Stuart, asked Secretary of the Navy Frank Knox to approve a program of exploration and test-well drilling in the reserve. The goal was to find out all about the area, including its potential for oil development. An initial reconnaissance party flew to the reserve on March 21; on returning, they recommended full-scale exploration. President Franklin Roosevelt approved on June 2 and the exploration program, known as Pet 4, began. The reserve itself was also commonly referred to as Pet 4.

With presidential approval, the Bureau of Yards and Docks mounted an expedition to further explore in Pet 4. Naval Construction Battalion (Seabees) Detachment 1058 was formed under the command of Lt. Cmdr. W.H. Rex. The USS *Spica*, an attack cargo ship, was assigned to carry men and equipment to Barrow. The SS *Jonathan Harrington*, a Liberty ship of the Alaska Steamship Co., and a PBY5-A Catalina flying boat completed the trio of craft in the expedition. The PBY was along to scout ice conditions along the route of the two ships. Between them, the *Spica* and

Harrington carried 196 Seabees and 235 stevedores, according to an article in the American Association of Petroleum Geologists' *Explorer*. Naval Reserve commander F.M. Kiley commanded the ship expedition.

On July 25, 1944, the expedition steamed out of Kodiak, headed for Dutch Harbor and the Bering Sea. On board the *Spica* as weatherman was Aerographer's Mate 1st Class Harold K. (Hal) Saur from Oakland, Calif. According to Saur's diary, the *Harrington* collided with a Russian steamer at Dutch and came away with a hole in her starboard side. On Aug. 2, the expedition reached Point Hope, which Saur described as "a dismal, lonesome looking spot with three or four wooden buildings and some tents dotting the landscape. Not a good liberty port, believe me."

Two days later the *Spica* reached Barrow. Saur went ashore for six hours, to talk with local radio- and weathermen. Of his contact with the Native residents of Barrow, Saur wrote: "All the Eskimos I saw could speak English. The small children kept chanting 'Hello, Hello.' Evidently they haven't learned goodbye yet as they didn't answer when I said 'goodbye.'"

The *Spica* and *Harrington* headed for Cape

The Search for Oil Continues

Barrow Natives enjoy treats while getting a closer look at the Spica *and its crew. (Courtesy of Harold K. Saur)*

CLOCKWISE, FROM BELOW:
The USS Spica, *an attack cargo ship, carried men and supplies to the North Slope to explore for oil during the war. (Courtesy of Harold K. Saur)*

California dreaming. The Navy looks over the beach at Barrow, August 1944. (Courtesy of Harold K. Saur)

From Saur's diary, August 12: "Finally started unloading our cargo here off Point Barrow. This isn't to be the main camp, but quite a bit of the cargo will be beached here until it is possible to move to the main campsite five miles southeast of Barrow village. Started working at once assembling the pontoon barges, neat rigs coming in three or four sections, bolted together, with a motor attached to one end." (Courtesy of Harold K. Saur)

Simpson, east of Barrow, which they reached on Aug. 6 after an 11-hour run from Barrow. The landing spot proved too muddy and damp so the ships returned to Barrow. For the next several weeks, the *Spica* and *Harrington* remained in the Barrow area, unloading their passengers and cargo, and dodging the ice as it moved onshore and offshore. The PBY sank in a storm that swept the Barrow area on Aug. 16, and the Navy sent another

PBY up from Kodiak to assist the ships on their southbound journey.

After the ships left the area, the Seabees completed the camps and runways, enabling the Pet 4 program to proceed. Though the expedition was a footnote in World War II history, the exploration for oil was part of an ongoing search on the North Slope that began shortly after the turn of the century and continues today. ■

TOP LEFT:
World War II seems far away for residents of Barrow in fall 1944. (Courtesy of Harold K. Saur)

LOWER LEFT:
From Saur's diary, August 21: "What a day! Started off calm enough with scattered skies....Became broken, then overcast about noon. At 1500 [3 pm] what we diagnosed as a cold front drove by with a sudden increase in wind from 15 to 30 knots. The sea became mighty rough with a ragged ugly sky and snow showers. All this happened faster than I'm writing this. A barge load of drill pipe and supplies was spilled in the heavy seas, with the other LCMs and barges running around the point to calmer weather." (Courtesy of Harold K. Saur)

Bibliography

Bush, Col. James D. *Narrative Report of Alaska Construction 1941-1944*. Anchorage: U.S. Army Engineers District Alaska, 1984.

Chandonnet, Fern, ed. *Alaska at War, 1941-1945*. Anchorage: Alaska at War Committee, 1995.

Cloe, John Haile. *The Aleutian Warriors. Part 1*. Missoula, Mont.: Anchorage Chapter - Air Force Association and Pictorial Histories Publishing Co., Inc., 1990.

Cohen, Stan. *The Forgotten War*. Missoula, Mont.: Pictorial Histories Publishing Co., 1981.

—. *The Forgotten War, Vol. Four*. Missoula, Mont.: Pictorial Histories Publishing Co., 1993.

Freeman, Elmer. *Those Navy Guys And Their PBY's*. Spokane, Wash.: Kedging Publishing Co., 1992.

"German Prisoners of War in Alaska." *The Alaska Journal*, Vol. 14, No. 4, 1984, page 16.

Marston, Muktuk. *Men of the Tundra*. New York: October House Inc., 1972.

Morgan, Lael, chief ed. *The Aleutians*. Vol. 7, No. 3. Anchorage: Alaska Geographic Society, 1980.

"Oilmen-Seabees Blazed Arctic Trail." *AAPG Explorer*, Vol. 15, No. 7, July 1994, page 20.

Reed, John C. *Exploration of Naval Petroleum Reserve No. 4 and Adjacent Areas, Northern Alaska, 1944-53, Part 1, History of the Exploration*. USGS Professional Paper 301. Washington D.C.: U.S. Government Printing Office, 1958.

Rennick, Penny, ed. *Islands of the Seals, The Pribilofs*. Vol. 9, No. 3. Anchorage: Alaska Geographic Society, 1982.

—. *Kodiak*. Vol. 19, No. 3. Anchorage: Alaska Geographic Society, 1992.

—. *Unalaska/Dutch Harbor*. Vol. 18, No. 4. Anchorage: Alaska Geographic Society, 1991.

Salisbury, C.A. *Soldiers of the Mists*. Missoula, Mont.: Pictorial Histories Publishing Co., 1992.

U.S. Naval Experience in the North Pacific During World War II. Naval Historical Center. Washington, D.C.: Dept. of the Navy, 1989.

Editor's note: *A well-known free-lance writer, Downs Matthews has written several books and numerous magazine articles and has traveled many times to the Arctic.*

Anatoly Sergeivich Gayevskyi sat us down at the cliff's edge 100 feet above a major walrus haul-out. "Don't talk loudly," he warned. "Don't stand up." We might startle them. "Take off your red anorak," he told photographer Dan Guravich. Too visible.

As state inspector of Russia's Arakamchechen Nature Reserve for walruses, Gayevskyi was protective of his charges. He feared that a wild stampede of alarmed animals into the Bering Sea might leave some animals injured or dead.

Not that the presence of walruses here was a secret. A hog-pen effluvium arose from the herd. Mud churned up by tons of clumsy bodies stained the green sea brown. Roars and bellows carried for miles. The sound, said a Danish farmer quoted by polar explorer and writer Peter Freuchen, was that of a thousand pigs turned loose with a thousand cows into a place where there was room for only half of them.

Cautiously, we peered over the cliff's edge to see 2,000 walruses sprawled on the shingle, like plastic bags of trash put out on a city sidewalk.

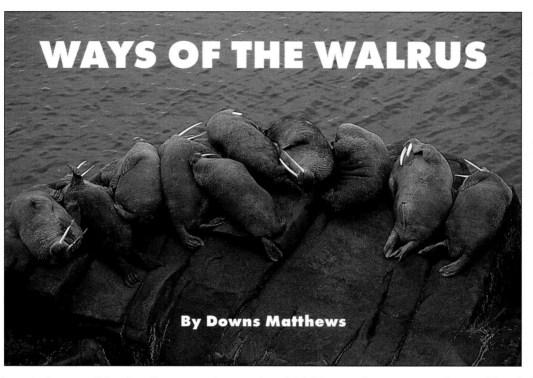

WAYS OF THE WALRUS

By Downs Matthews

Round Island State Game Sanctuary, off the north shore of Bristol Bay, is Alaska's best-known walrus-viewing area. In 1995, an estimated 7,000 bull walrus used the island, primarily in the summer. Also in 1995, for the first time since statehood in 1959, the Alaska Board of Game allowed Natives living in the Togiak area to kill 10 walrus in the sanctuary. (Harry M. Walker)

Smelly, warty, inert tubs of blubber, walruses lack the status of charismatic megafauna. No droll creatures these, consorting with carpenters and discussing cabbages with kings. They were 2,000-pound, 10-foot slugs determinedly doing what walruses do best, which is to sleep and bicker.

The walruses using this beach, 90 percent of them adult bulls, were part of some 20,000 animals loosely congregated in this vicinity. While these slept, others miles out to sea grazed clam beds 300 feet down in the clear, cold water. For each one visible at the surface, seven more would be browsing busily on the bottom.

Through binoculars, I watched an individual walrus surface and exhale noisily after 10 minutes of feeding. The animal would rest on his back, tusks up, with paddlelike foreflippers folded on his chest. Rolling over, he would arch his back and dive head first, thrusting downward with his foreflippers. Then with alternate strokes of his hindflippers, he would swim down to the bottom to feed.

For centuries, conventional wisdom insisted that walruses dug up clams by plowing clam beds with their tusks. But the late Dr. Francis H. (Bud) Fay said no. As a biologist with the Institute of Marine Science in Fairbanks, Alaska, Fay wrote *Ecology and Biology of the Pacific Walrus.* (1982). Before his death in 1994, Fay told me:

A feeding walrus floats face down at the seafloor, tail up, steadying himself with his front flippers. He roots in the sandy bottom like a hog, probing with the stiff hairs of his wiry

mustache for clams. Finding mollusks, he scoops up a mouthful with his large muscular lips.

Depressing his powerful pistonlike tongue to create a full atmosphere of suction, the walrus vacuums the little bivalves right out of their shells. Opening his jaws, he spits out the empty shells and then swallows the meat. If the clams are large and fat, a hundred may fill him up, but if they are small, he may gobble up to 6,000 before reaching his limit.

That may take him up to a week, which means that walruses need special equipment to sleep in the deep. I watched one sleeping walrus as he hung vertically in the water, held up by air in balloonlike pouches in his neck. As he bobbed in the waves, his nostrils opened and closed like the valve in a snorkel.

After a week's clamming, a walrus needs a rest. I watched one surfeited animal swim toward

TOP: *Walrus eyes maintain a bloodshot appearance when the animals are in the water. When they come ashore, their eyes change to brown. (Dr. Nikita Ovsyanikov)*

LEFT: *A Yup'ik walrus hunter scrapes the ivory tusks of a butchered walrus. The walrus meat is used to feed foxes at government-run fur farms. (Downs Matthews)*

shore, porpoising with head and tusks down, foreflippers folded along his sides, and stroking alternately with hindflippers. He stopped in shallow water to rest. In the sun's warmth, his grayish brown hide gradually turned rose-pink as blood suffused the surface. His bloodshot eyes gradually lost their red marble look and turned brown.

Tired and grouchy, this walrus wanted nothing more than to stretch his 10 feet of bulk onto the rocks and sleep with the other guys. He eased up to the first row at the water's edge and tried to squeeze in. Objecting to having a ton of weight draped over his chest, one of the supine sleepers awakened and protested with anguished roars. Pushed off, the newcomer mashed a neighbor's flipper. Rudely awakened, he of the flattened fin foot reared back and displayed formidable tusks 2 feet long. He jabbed them angrily into the back of yet a fourth sleeper. With gravelly bellows and belching barks, the gouged victim remonstrated. Soon six walruses were awake, waving their tusks, and demanding their rights. But somehow, the crowd accommodated the newcomer, who displayed some remarkable tusks of his own. Slowly the bickering subsided until the next weary traveler struggled in farther down the shingle. Then it began again.

Such is the good life in the Arakamchechen old boys' club, or any of the other 11 haul-outs along the Chukotsk Peninsula.

The ladies understandably leave the men to their snores and arguments, and migrate north toward the permanent ice pack in the Chukchi Sea. Along the way, perhaps a third of them give birth in the water to yard-long, 120-pound calves.

Throughout the summer, mothers of newborns, yearlings and two-year-olds stay together on ice floes until time to rejoin the males with the onslaught of winter. A female can delay fetal growth for so long that her pregnancy may last from 15 to 16 months. She'll continue to suckle her calf for up to two years.

Males and females reunite in early winter and stay together in small family groups on pans of ice or on small island haul-outs called uglis. In February, after males have fought a few rounds to settle the question of who gets the honors, females with two-year-old calves accept mates, and the cycle begins again.

Gregarious, tolerant of each other, protective of their friends and relatives, walruses seem deserving of more sympathy than they usually get. "They are," Freuchen wrote in 1958 in *The Arctic Year*, "the most sensible animal in the sea."

Nevertheless, *morsh*, as the Russians call them, are not to be trifled with. Threatened, walruses defend themselves and their families vigorously. Two-foot-long tusks make fearsome weapons. The ivory is so strong that a 2,000-pound walrus can hook his tusks onto the edge of an ice floe and lift himself right out of the water. Thus their Latin name, *Odobenus rosmarus*, the sea-horse that walks with its teeth.

"In the water," wrote biologist F. G. Jackson in his diary, published in 1899, "walruses, especially bulls, may be really dangerous when irritated, and often, quite unprovoked, will go for a boat and with their enormous tusks, tear a hole in it and sink it." Jackson and companions conducted research for three years in Russia's Franz Josef Land, an archipelago straddling the Arctic Circle between the Arctic Ocean and the Barents Sea.

"Once...a companion and I were standing at the floe edge watching a small herd of cows and cubs disporting themselves a short distance off in the water. Suddenly a large bull put his head above the water and came straight for us,

RIGHT: *Yup'ik walrus hunter Alilik, from Novo Chaplino, shows how a walrus harpoon is rigged. (Downs Matthews)*

BELOW: *Commercial walrus hunters from Novo Chaplino have killed a walrus near Yttygran Island in northeastern Russia. (Downs Matthews)*

bellowing angrily, and proceeded to clamber on to the ice with the intention of turning us off it. My companion fired at him and he fell back into the water."

Much of a walrus's bluster may be no more than bluff, as an incident reported in 1925 by Capt. Thierry Mallet in *Plain Tales of the Far North* suggests.

"We were forging through the ice of Hudson Straits on an auxiliary schooner. There were on board a lot of husky dogs which we were transferring from one trading station to another.

"One morning the man in the crow's nest saw a small herd of walrus asleep on the ice. Creeping up slowly, we got up to a hundred yards from them before they took any notice of the ship.

"The meat was needed for the dogs. Firing a volley we killed two of the huge animals outright. The rest of the herd dived and scattered. Manoeuvering alongside the pan, we put one man of the crew overboard to rope the carcasses to be hoisted on deck with the winch.

During the fall of 1990, several dozen polar bears were observed on the gravel spit of Wrangel Island's Cape Blossom waiting for opportunities to hunt the walrus swimming just offshore. (Dr. Nikita Ovsyanikov)

For example, in 1990, a year when the permanent ice pack retreated and left Wrangel Island ice free, around 170,000 walruses went ashore on its rarely exposed beaches. Dr. Nikita Ovsyanikov, at that time deputy director for science at the Wrangel Island Nature Preserve, reported that polar bears were also forced ashore. They tried unsuccessfully to catch and kill adult walruses, whose tough hide proved impenetrable. One 1,000-pound bear climbed onto the back of a 2,000-pound walrus and rode it into the water. The walrus submerged and surfaced beside the swimming bear, tusks up and ready to fight. The intimidated bear wisely returned to dry land.

Polar bears took a few calves, Ovsyanikov said. But that was nothing compared to the bounty provided when an airplane buzzed a Wrangel Island beach on which 30,000 walruses had hauled out. In the resulting scramble for the

"It happened that the sailor who went over the side...had never been in the North. He was very keen and excited. While he was busy tying a rope around each animal's head under the tusks, a big bull walrus, which had probably been wounded in the body a few minutes before, suddenly came up to the surface beside the pan. With one heave, the enormous animal jumped clean out of the water to the ice a few feet from the sailor whose back was turned. Everyone on board was terrified. Nobody dared to shoot for fear of hitting the man.

"The walrus shook his head and seemed ready to plunge his tusks right in the middle of the man's back....

"Feeling the animal's breath on him, the sailor turned round. 'Get out of here, you ugly thing!' he shouted, and with that he slapped him right across the jaw with the back of his hand. The walrus gave a grunt, slid backwards over the edge of the pan and vanished into the depths of the sea."

An inch-thick hide padded with 4 inches of blubber provides the morsh with formidable armor against injury from such predators as polar bears.

water, 104 walruses were killed. As many as 60 polar bears feasted on their carcasses for weeks, said Ovsyanikov.

Neither tusks nor hide can turn away the teeth of an orca, or killer whale, however.

Gayevskyi, a graduate of the Magadan Zootechnical Institute and inspector of the Arakamchechen Reserve for nine years, told me that on August 10, 1993, he watched as a pod of about 50 walruses approached the island after feeding. They were cruising at 6 or 7 knots when a pair of adult male orcas charged into the pod and cut 10 walruses out of the pack. The orcas then turned on the isolated animals and chopped them into pieces with their interlocking knifelike teeth.

"An orca would take a full-grown morsh by the head and toss it 30 feet into the air," Gayevskyi said. "The orcas jumped out of the water and crashed down on top of the morsh. Hectares of blood stained the water's surface."

As an orca can eat no more than 200 pounds of meat, most of the killing took place in a feeding frenzy.

The remaining walruses dashed for land at their top speed of 20 knots as the orcas harassed the slower animals.

When we examined the walrus herd at Cape Kygynin the next day, we saw several that had lost flippers. One had a great crescent-shaped bite wound in its side.

Nor do walruses have much in the way of defenses against the ancient skills of Native hunters.

Ingata and Alilik, half-brothers from the village of Novo Chaplino, have hunted walruses as long as either can remember. Alilik showed me his harpoon, a wooden pole perhaps 5 feet long, with a socket in one end to accept an iron shaft. The small steel harpoon head, fitted to the end of the shaft, was S-shaped, about 6 inches long, with a sharp metal triangle slotted into one end. A light rope was roved through the center. The device was designed to turn at right angles to the entry hole when thrust into the animal's body. At the other end of the rope, Alilik tied a plastic float. Hunters work from long wooden whale boats powered with outboard motors. They try to approach as closely as possible to a swimming animal so that the harpooner, standing in the bow, can't miss.

"You aim for any soft place," Ingata said, "not his head. First you strike him. Then you throw the float overboard. The morsh will dive to the bottom but the float makes him tired. He has to come up. Then we shoot him in the head."

Hunters tow the dead animal to shore and roll it up on the shingle. There, the boat crew butchers it with long knives. The head is severed and skinned. Using a hand ax, a man chops through the heavy upper jaw bone to free the tusks.

The meat is divided according to traditional rules of the hunt. The crew that first harpooned the animal owns it. And the man who threw

A female bear and her two cubs-of-the-year eat the remains of a walrus calf killed by another bear. Only a few mature polar bears, the most experienced, can hunt walruses on the beach successfully. Other bears are hangers-on, looking for remains. (Dr. Nikita Ovsyanikov)

the harpoon gets the choice cuts, the head and tusks and the front left quarter, including the heart. The rest is divided among other members of the crew.

"We eat all of it," Ingata said. "Everything but the tusks."

Alilik offered me a pot of walrus meat that he had been cooking on a camp stove fashioned out of a gasoline-fueled blow torch. "He was swimming just three days ago," he said.

The meat put me in mind of coarse beef marinated in cod liver oil. The skin, eaten as a delicacy called *manguna*, was served in 1-inch cubes having the consistency of grainy cork.

"It will stay in your stomach a long time," Alilik told me.

"Walrus meat is strong meat. It makes a man strong," Ingata said. And fortunately so, for it takes strength and courage to attack and kill a huge, well-armed animal in its own element.

Ingata saved his crew one day when an angry walrus surfaced unexpectedly beside the boat

A mature male polar bear (left) rushes to attack a newly formed rookery. Immediately the walruses turned back to the surf, splashing the water in their attempt to get away. Right, a mature female walrus that failed to escape before the polar bear reached her turns to confront the bear. The walrus stopped the bear by showing that she is willing to use her tusks for defense. (Both, Dr. Nikita Ovsyanikov)

and hooked his tusks over the gunwale. Just as the boat was swamping, Ingata kicked the animal in the head and it jumped away.

When a female walrus attacked his boat, a hunter from Sireniki seized her tusks with his hands and held up her head.

"He is really a tough man," Alilik said.

The hunter's brother seized the boat's rifle and shot between the man's hands to kill the animal.

"It was a great joke," added Alilik. "They said they wouldn't need to harpoon morsh any more. Just grab them by their tusks."

Joaquim, also from Sireniki, was at the helm as his crew chased a swimming walrus that submerged. Joaquim stood up to look for the animal. At that moment, the walrus burst from the water at the stern and plunged its tusks into the seat where Joaquim had been sitting, ripping it out. Unaware of what had happened, Joaquim tried to sit on the missing seat and fell into the boat's bilges.

"Everybody laughed," Ingata said. Joaquim gave thanks to his ancestors. "They knew the morsh would attack so they made me stand up and that saved me."

Yup'ik hunters are adamant in their belief that if a mother walrus is killed, her calf must be killed also. If left alive, they believe, the calf will grow up to be a rogue that feeds exclusively on seals and will try to kill people as well.

"The tusks of a rogue morsh grow straight and sharp instead of curved," Alilik said. "They kill with them. Rogues are very dangerous for boats and people. When our hunters went out on the edge of the ice, rogues would break through the ice and try to kill them. One hunter was chased by a rogue who thought the man was a seal. The morsh was very surprised that the seal could run so fast."

But scientist Fay cautioned that the rogue walrus story is part fact and part fiction. "Hundreds of examinations of stomach contents tell us that many walruses eat seals occasionally,

and some may make a regular practice of it, especially when and where other foods are scarce," he told me.

For each walrus taken, hunters estimate that they wound three others that get away. Some recover. Some die.

"We catch many with scars," Ingata said. "We find bullets and harpoon heads inside."

Ovsyanikov came upon a wounded walrus on a Wrangel Island beach, still alive, sitting with its head slumped nearly to the ground, one tusk shot off, bullet wounds in its head and neck. Blood dripped steadily from its nose and mouth and formed a long slimy red icicle to the ground.

"The morsh could not move and was waiting for death," Ovsyanikov said. "I would have put it out of its misery, but I had no gun."

Undoubtedly, walruses have killed hunters, too. But accounts of such killings often turn out to be fables.

Beth Thomson, a biologist with the Canada Department of Fisheries and Oceans in Winnipeg, Manitoba, heard at a meeting of trappers and commercial fishermen that a walrus had leaped out of the water onto an ice pan in Resolute Bay where it had caught and killed a native child.

But Bezal Jesudason, the North's leading outfitter, who lives in Resolute, said that is not what happened.

On July 9, 1974, a group of Eskimo youngsters was playing at the edge of the ice. Among them was 12-year-old Jackie Naqtai. The boy accidentally fell in the water and drowned. His body was never found.

"Walruses had been seen in the vicinity," Jesudason said, "but they had nothing to do with the kid's death."

Walruses are very protective of each other, Jesudason reports. "When hunters wound one, others will try to help it by holding it up in the water and driving away the attacker. That's why the Inuit prefer to hunt walrus only while they are hauled out on the ice."

In Alexandra Fjord, an area of Canada's Ellesmere Island near Buchanan Bay, wildlife photographer Fred Bruemmer approached a walrus family in an inflatable boat. An adult male charged and punctured one of the boat's five air chambers with its tusks. The occupants weren't harmed, Bruemmer said, but they had a long, wet ride home in the damaged boat.

When threatened, mother walruses will clasp their babies to their breasts with their foreflippers and swim away.

"I have seen pathetic sights of mothers with their cubs, endeavoring to shield them from danger by clasping them with their flippers and swimming with them in their embrace," wrote Jackson in his diary.

Native hunters continue to pursue walruses, although hunting pressure is far less today. For example, at the beginning of the 19th century, there were perhaps a million walruses in the Atlantic and Pacific, says Dr. Ovsyanikov. But merciless hunting reduced the Atlantic population to near extinction. The blubber of a walrus was valued for the 15 gallons of lubricating oil that could be rendered from it.

Next in line, the Pacific population was on its way out as well when the timely intervention of cheap petroleum lubricants forced animal-based oils and greases off the market.

Scientists say the world's walrus population in 1975 probably exceeded 270,000 animals, about 90 percent of them Pacific walruses in

Bull walrus rest along this sandy beach on Arakamchechen Island, in the Bering Sea north of Provideniya. The site is one of several being studied by a joint United States-Russia team for a proposed international park on both sides of Bering Strait. (Leslie Kerr, USFWS)

the Bering and Chukchi seas. A limited census of Atlantic walruses conducted in 1988 by Pierre Richard, who works in walrus management for the Canada Department of Fisheries and Oceans, counted around 11,000 animals in Canadian waters.

A joint Russian-American census carried out in 1985 put the Pacific population at 250,000 animals. In 1990, under extremely unfavorable conditions that precluded any accurate count of Pacific walruses, biologists guessed their number at somewhere around 200,000.

Are walrus populations, then, in danger?

"History teaches us," Fay said, "that the harvesting of walruses, especially females, from ships that can go anywhere and carry large loads can be devastating to walrus populations. But walruses are no longer hunted with ships. Subsistence hunting by Natives continues, but the limited capacity and short range of their small boats prevents Native hunters from subtracting enough animals from the population to endanger it. Subsistence hunting, especially in Alaska, has declined greatly since 1987."

Furthermore, subsistence hunting is directed largely at males. Since walruses are long-lived animals with life expectancies of 40 years, the herds can handle losses as long as females are not taken in large numbers.

As of 1994, Fay told me, Pacific walrus numbers have stabilized. Yet he was worried that walruses don't seem to be getting enough to eat. Studies indicate that the walrus population is getting older. Birth rates are down. Adults are thinner than they used to be, and they are eating things like sea anemones and jellyfish that were once ignored. Walrus predation on seals has risen from 10 to 100 times what it used to be four decades ago. The problem may be related to a food supply that seems to be shrinking for reasons not clearly understood.

Conceivably, a food shortage could have a more serious impact on walrus numbers than the commercial killing of them, which admittedly, still takes place on both sides of the Bering Sea.

Since 1982, Siberian Eskimos and Maritime Chukchi have worked as commercial walrus hunters for state-owned fox farms in the Chukotka Autonomous Republic. The Eskimos of northeastern Russia are Yup'ik-speakers who populate the coast as far north as Arakamchechen Island; the Maritime Chukchi are an ancient culture of Yakut speakers living on the Chukchi Peninsula. Each Native community receives a quota ranging from 200 to 400 walruses, depending on how many hunters live there. Native hunters say from 10,000 to 12,000 walruses are slaughtered each year to feed silver foxes whose pelts have little value in the world fur market.

"Most walrus hunting is not for subsistence," Ingata told me. "It is just killing. If the fox farms weren't here, the walrus population would be much larger, like in olden days. If governments in Russia and the United States would prohibit the sale of ivory, that would help," Ingata said.

To study walrus behavior and the effects of hunting pressure on the herds, Ovsyanikov and his biologist wife, Irina, camped on a Wrangel Island headland overlooking a walrus haul-out. As they watched, Chukchi walrus hunters entered the bay in two angyaqs (skin boats) powered by outboard motors. The hunters saw the Russian biologists and came ashore to visit.

"They were very gracious and kind," Ovsyanikov recalls. "They shared their tea and food, and offered to give us a ride back to their village whenever we wanted to go."

Ovsyanikov asked about the newly introduced hunting quotas on walrus. The hunters said they were in complete agreement with the system. It was wise to conserve walruses, they said, and added that since they had already taken their quota of 100 animals, they would be taking no more the rest of the year.

Their visit concluded, the hunters got back in their boats and motored away.

Ovsyanikov climbed to the crest of the headland to watch them go.

"They were no sooner around the headland and out of sight of our camp than a walrus surfaced nearby," he recalled. "Both boats took chase. They fired 16 shots at the swimming animal. It sank to the bottom. They motored on and left it to die."

They had been hunters all their lives, Ovsyanikov said, just like their Beringian ancestors in a hunting culture 16,000 years old. "For them, the hunting instinct was just too strong to resist." ■

TOP AND MIDDLE RIGHT:
A mature male bear tries to seize an exhausted female walrus that was lying separately in front of the main rookery. However, even a weakened, starved walrus is too strong an adversary for the bear, which was unsuccessful in this attack. (Both, Dr. Nikita Ovsyanikov)

LOWER RIGHT:
A female walrus pushes her calf along an ice floe. When in danger, a female will hug her young with her flippers and try to swim away. (Lloyd Lowry, ADFG)

Doing Time in the Promised Land

By Paul Kallmes
Photos courtesy of the author

Editor's note: An avid mountain photographer and manager of a gallery specializing in photographs of mountains, Paul Kallmes tries to climb at least one major route each year, whether snow and ice or a rock wall. Paul notes that he "has been hit by lightning three times and fallen off lots of rocks, but still hasn't learned his lesson."

A complex chain of events leads a person to try to climb a mountain. Whatever that particular chain was for me, in mid-April 1994 my partner, Joe Lackey, and I found ourselves sitting at Gulf Air in Yakutat, rapidly re-orienting our ambitions because of reports of nightmarish glacier conditions on Mount St. Elias, our original destination. These conditions change all our plans and send us to Mount Fairweather. Nothing counts as much as adaptability in the mountains.

The astonishment of a first-timer to the Fairweather Range devours me on the flight in. I have never dreamed of peaks like these. Only photos could do them justice, and even they fall short. We get dropped off at our base camp at 5,000 feet on a glacier, with Kurt

Joe Lackey crouches below an ice wave.

Gloyer's Cessna echoing long after it disappears oceanward. Joe and I are left facing our new ambition, the eastern south ridge of Mount Fairweather, which climbs 10,000 feet out of a glacier.

We are completely alone. There is not a lot of traffic in these mountains, even though the first ascent of Fairweather was in 1931. If they could do it then... the climber's ego built from time and technology lifts our spirits as we simultaneously unpack our base camp and load up our packs for the climb. Up at 2:30 a.m., away at 4:30. I will never adapt to these early morning starts. At least the wall above is beyond scrutiny. Skis stashed, our line chosen, Joe starts up. This snow is ugly, thigh deep, and since we're on an avalanche cone, it would be nice to get off it quickly. We struggle about three hours and gain a thousand feet, at which point wispy clouds assume the proportions of a major storm, at least in our minds. We drop most of our gear and speed to base camp at nearly eight times our upward velocity. A quiet ski back to camp gives us both ample time to reflect on our commitment to this route.

Of course, the next day is glorious. A ski trip up the valley shows us some really serious snow walls, putting ours sufficiently in perspective so that we are packing again that evening. We will try twice but not three times, so this attempt will have to work. The packs are lighter but no easier to carry in the gray light of morning. Nine hours and 3,700 vertical feet later, we are chopping a bivouac out of the base of an overhanging boulder. We belayed perhaps five times today. The tension is often as palpable as the cold.

Morning brings high winds, clear sky, blazing sun and a knife-edged ridge with a 3,000-foot drop to the glacier: scary stuff first thing in the morning. Mutual motivation is what this is all about, because in a lifetime of feeling small in the mountains, neither Joe nor I has every felt quite this small. We can still make out the tracks around our camp, and I at least cannot resist the temptation of picking out a descent route, should one become necessary. I do not ask Joe if he's doing the same, although I find out later that he is.

The climbing is fantastically varied, giving us everything but real protection. Steep ice, steep snow, steep and loose rock, the rope is both our safety and the greatest threat to it. If one of us falls, then the other goes and we start praying that the rope catches on something. The other option is to jump off the other side of the ridge, if possible. Eight hours of penance rewards us with

1,000 more vertical feet, a rather deepened sense of commitment and even a comfortable home for the night.

It is freezing here. Joe, a North Carolina native, informs me that he hates, *hates*, cold weather. I love cold weather, but

Below, Paul Kallmes climbs the steep route between the first and the second promised land and at right poses at the climbing team's second bivouac.

Kurt Gloyer of Gulf Air has landed his Cessna on Fairweather Glacier to deposit the gear for Joe Lackey and Paul Kallmes for their ascent of Mount Fairweather. Their proposed route generally follows the top of the rock buttress and ridges that rise from lower left to upper right.

when pressed, I admit that I don't know exactly what we are doing here. We channel our dislike of the present into reaching a major landmark ahead, a huge, curving plateau we have named the Promised Land. The now-routine, early-morning, empty-stomach climbing up steep snow and ice deposits us at a 75-degree snow wall below our Promised Land.

Neither of us is experienced at pilgrimages, but we are learning.

Joe outdoes himself on the detestable snow slopes below today's mecca, only to reach what must be one of the more disappointing promised lands. For three hours we plod up alternating thin ice and hard snow with no reasonable protection, not even a ridge to jump from, should one of us stumble. Lunch is a rock-hard Power Bar®. The afternoon starts with an unpleasant gully full of Damoclean blocks, and the rope is starting to look awfully thin at .35 of an inch. I emerge from the gully intact, but now confronted by the most widely corniced ridge I have ever seen.

The next hour is tense and intense, weaving in and out of rock towers, over unstable snow bridges, marveling at the 5,000 feet straight down to the glacier off my right side, a total of one sling around a rock for protection in 800 torturous feet. I eventually reach a two-foot-wide ridge that feels like the autobahn. A final 500 feet, a quick drop up to my waist in a crevasse, and I get my well-earned collapse into a snowbank. Joe drags me up the last 400 feet to a bivouac, just below the second Promised Land. My arms ache to recall the two hours spent hacking a platform out of a substance that resembles ice but is actually a clear alloy of titanium. Remarkably enough, I sleep almost six hours, inches from a void.

We cannot escape this ugly site quickly enough. The daily deep-freeze of my toes brings tears to my eyes as I belay Joe up. I don't bother to tell him that the anchor, two axes plunged into soft snow, wouldn't hold more than a tug. He vaults past me to the second promised land, as unfulfilling as the first. Two hours of tiptoeing and complaining and we have finished the ridge. Tonight's bivouac, on the west side of the mountain at 13,000 feet, is a welcome change from the previous one, warm, sunny and dug in below an overhanging wave of ice.

Next day to the top. We make it by 1:00 p.m. Clear as can be, cold as can be, the Pacific and the most spectacular array of summits imaginable constitute our reward. All the big peaks are visible: Crillon, Salisbury, Logan, St. Elias, Kennedy, Hubbard and hundreds more. The wind makes it too cold to loiter, so we stomp down to camp to bask in sunny, 80-degree temperatures, an ambition fulfilled. Only 8,000 feet of descending the next day separate us from the real promised land, that firm and flat safety of places near enough to the mountains to watch them but far enough away not to be in constant fear of harm or worse. ■

BELOW: *Joe Lackey has reached the 15,300-summit of Mount Fairweather.*

RIGHT: *At the third bivouac on the west side of Mount Fairweather, the climbers pitch their tent between a rock wall and a void. A glacier flows from the mountains to the Pacific Ocean in the distance.*

Index

ALASKA GEOGRAPHIC. Back Issues

The North Slope, Vol. 1, No. 1. Out of print.

One Man's Wilderness, Vol. 1, No. 2. Out of print.

Admiralty...Island in Contention, Vol. 1, No. 3. $7.50.

Fisheries of the North Pacific, Vol. 1, No. 4. Out of print.

Alaska-Yukon Wild Flowers, Vol. 2, No. 1. Out of print.

Richard Harrington's Yukon, Vol. 2, No. 2. Out of print.

Prince William Sound, Vol. 2, No. 3. Out of print.

Yakutat: The Turbulent Crescent, Vol. 2, No. 4. Out of print.

Glacier Bay: Old Ice, New Land, Vol. 3, No. 1. Out of print.

The Land: Eye of the Storm, Vol. 3, No. 2. Out of print.

Richard Harrington's Antarctic, Vol. 3, No. 3. $17.95.

The Silver Years, Vol. 3, No. 4. $17.95.

Alaska's Volcanoes, Vol. 4, No. 1. Out of print.

The Brooks Range, Vol. 4, No. 2. Out of print.

STATEMENT OF OWNERSHIP, MANAGEMENT & CIRCULATION

ALASKA GEOGRAPHIC® is a quarterly publication, home office at P.O. Box 93370, Anchorage, AK 99509. Editor is Penny Rennick. Publisher and owner is The Alaska Geographic Society, a non-profit Alaska organization, P.O. Box 93370, Anchorage, AK 99509. *ALASKA GEOGRAPHIC®* has a membership of 6,046.

Total number of copies	**10,000**
Paid and/or requested circulation	
Sales through dealers, etc.	0
Mail subscription	6,046
Total paid and/or requested circulation	6,046
Free distribution	0
Total distribution	6,046
Copies not distributed (office use, returns, etc.)	3,954
TOTAL	**10,000**

I certify that the statement above is correct and complete.

—Vickie Staples
Circulation/Database Manager

Kodiak: Island of Change, Vol. 4, No. 3. Out of print.

Wilderness Proposals, Vol. 4, No. 4. Out of print.

Cook Inlet Country, Vol. 5, No. 1. Out of print.

Southeast: Alaska's Panhandle, Vol. 5, No. 2. Out of print.

Bristol Bay Basin, Vol. 5, No. 3. Out of print.

Alaska Whales and Whaling, Vol. 5, No. 4. $19.95.

Yukon-Kuskokwim Delta, Vol. 6, No. 1. Out of print.

Aurora Borealis, Vol. 6, No. 2. $19.95.

Alaska's Native People, Vol. 6, No. 3. $24.95.

The Stikine River, Vol. 6, No. 4. $17.95.

Alaska's Great Interior, Vol. 7, No. 1. $17.95.

Photographic Geography of Alaska, Vol. 7, No. 2. Out of print.

The Aleutians, Vol. 7, No. 3. Out of print.

Klondike Lost, Vol. 7, No. 4. Out of print.

Wrangell-Saint Elias, Vol. 8, No. 1. Out of print.

Alaska Mammals, Vol. 8, No. 2. Out of print.

The Kotzebue Basin, Vol. 8, No. 3. Out of print.

Alaska National Interest Lands, Vol. 8, No. 4. $17.95.

Alaska's Glaciers, Vol. 9, No. 1. Revised 1993. $19.95.

Sitka and Its Ocean/Island World, Vol. 9, No. 2. Out of print.

Islands of the Seals: The Pribilofs, Vol. 9, No. 3. $17.95.

Alaska's Oil/Gas & Minerals Industry, Vol. 9, No. 4. $17.95.

Adventure Roads North, Vol. 10, No. 1. $17.95.

Anchorage and the Cook Inlet Basin, Vol. 10, No. 2. $17.95.

Alaska's Salmon Fisheries, Vol. 10, No. 3. $17.95.

Up the Koyukuk, Vol. 10, No. 4. $17.95.

Nome: City of the Golden Beaches, Vol. 11, No. 1. $17.95.

Alaska's Farms and Gardens, Vol. 11, No. 2. $17.95.

Chilkat River Valley, Vol. 11, No. 3. $17.95.

Alaska Steam, Vol. 11, No. 4. $17.95.

Northwest Territories, Vol. 12, No. 1. $17.95.

Alaska's Forest Resources, Vol. 12, No. 2. $17.95.

Alaska Native Arts and Crafts, Vol. 12, No. 3. $22.95.

Our Arctic Year, Vol. 12, No. 4. $17.95.

Where Mountains Meet the Sea, Vol. 13, No. 1. $17.95.

Backcountry Alaska, Vol. 13, No. 2. $17.95.

British Columbia's Coast, Vol. 13, No. 3. $17.95.

Lake Clark/Lake Iliamna, Vol. 13, No. 4. Out of print.

Dogs of the North, Vol. 14, No. 1. $17.95.

South/Southeast Alaska, Vol. 14, No. 2. Out of print.

Alaska's Seward Peninsula, Vol. 14, No. 3. $17.95.

The Upper Yukon Basin, Vol. 14, No. 4. $17.95.

Glacier Bay: Icy Wilderness, Vol. 15, No. 1. Out of print.

Dawson City, Vol. 15, No. 2. $17.95.

Denali, Vol. 15, No. 3. $19.95.

The Kuskokwim River, Vol. 15, No. 4. $17.95.

Katmai Country, Vol. 16, No. 1. $17.95.

North Slope Now, Vol. 16, No. 2. $17.95.

The Tanana Basin, Vol. 16, No. 3. $17.95.

The Copper Trail, Vol. 16, No. 4. $17.95.

The Nushagak Basin, Vol. 17, No. 1. $17.95.

Juneau, Vol. 17, No. 2. Out of print.

The Middle Yukon River, Vol. 17, No. 3. $17.95.

The Lower Yukon River, Vol. 17, No. 4. $17.95.

Alaska's Weather, Vol. 18, No. 1. $17.95.

Alaska's Volcanoes, Vol. 18, No. 2. $17.95.

Admiralty Island: Fortress of Bears, Vol. 18, No. 3. $17.95.

Unalaska/Dutch Harbor, Vol. 18, No. 4. $17.95.

Skagway: A Legacy of Gold, Vol. 19, No. 1. $18.95.

ALASKA: The Great Land, Vol. 19, No. 2. $18.95.

Kodiak, Vol. 19, No. 3. $18.95.

Alaska's Railroads, Vol. 19, No. 4. $18.95.

Prince William Sound, Vol. 20, No. 1. $18.95.

Southeast Alaska, Vol. 20, No. 2. $19.95.

Arctic National Wildlife Refuge, Vol. 20, N| $18.95.

Alaska's Bears, Vol. 20, No. 4. $18.95.

The Alaska Peninsula, Vol. 21, No. 1. $19.|

The Kenai Peninsula, Vol. 21, No. 2. $19.9

People of Alaska, Vol. 21, No. 3. $19.95.

Prehistoric Alaska, Vol. 21, No. 4. $19.95.|

Fairbanks, Vol. 22, No. 1. $19.95.|

The Aleutian Islands, Vol. 22, No. 2. $19.9

Rich Earth: Alaska's Mineral Industry, Vo| No. 3. $19.95.

ALL PRICES SUBJECT TO CHANG|

Your $39 membership in The Alaska Geographic Society includes four subsequ| issues of *ALASKA GEOGRAPHIC®*, the Society's award-winning quarterly. Please| add $10 per year for non-U.S. membership|

Additional membership information and| free catalog are available on request. Sing| *ALASKA GEOGRAPHIC®* back issues are| also available. For back issues add $2 pos| and handling per copy for Book Rate; $4 | for Priority Mail. Inquire for non-U.S. posta| rates. To order back issues send check or| money order (U.S. funds, please) or credit| card information (including expiration date| daytime phone number) and titles desired|

ALASKA GEOGRAPHIC.|
Box 93370 • Anchorage, AK 99509-|
Phone (907) 562-0164; Fax (907) 562-|
e-mail: akgeo@anc.ak.net

NEXT ISSUE: *Anchorage*, Vol. 23, No| It's Alaska's biggest and boldest city,:| urban outpost on the Last Frontier. T| state's commerce, transportation, co| munications and services center arou| this city on upper Cook Inlet that| railroad built, a war expanded, an| industry fueled and government and| service industry sustain. Readers '| enjoy this close look at a city of pione| and boomers, where there's money to| made, a good life to be had, an in| pendence to fight for and where Alask| "only a short drive away." To memb| early 1996, with index. Price $19.95.